Ten Things Christians Wish Jesus Hadn't Taught

Ten Things Christians Wish Jesus Hadn't Taught

And Other Reasons to Question His Words

To: Cory English
"Keep the faith.... away!"

David Madison

Ph.D. Biblical Studies

Ten Things Christians Wish Jesus Hadn't Taught: And Other Reasons to Question His Words

David Madison
www.BadThingsJesusTaught.com

Tim Sledge, Editor

Cover Design by M. A. Rehman
Using a Public Domain Photo of
Rembrandt's *Head of Christ*
Back Cover Author Photo by Andrea Reese

Printed in the United States of America

First Edition: August 2021

Insighting Growth Publications
Houston, Texas
www.IGrowPub.com

ISBN-13: 978-1-7333520-8-6 (Paperback)
ISBN-13: 978-1-7333520-9-3 (E-Book)

Foreword

What are we to do when we run across something in the Bible that sounds goofy, deranged, or even downright evil? Perhaps what one needs is an informed guide, and for that, an earnest seeker could hardly find a better one than Dr. David Madison.

As a teenager in the prairie-flatlands of northern Indiana, while other kids were out shooting hoops, young David was attending church and voraciously reading his mother's hefty 12-volume *Interpreter's Bible,* a serious collection of scripture commentary and exegesis, written by biblical scholars for ministers. His interest in the Bible carried over to college, where he became active in the Methodist Wesley Foundation for students and gravitated toward the ministry with the goal of teaching Bible as a college-level academic.

After graduating from college, David went to the Boston University School of Theology, the alma mater of Dr. Martin Luther King. There he gained reading proficiency in biblical Hebrew and Greek, and, to keep up with advances in scholarship, he studied French and German as well. He completed his Ph.D. in Biblical studies while serving two parishes as a Methodist minister.

Few Christians are as well-schooled in their faith or as

well-armed against threats to faith as David Madison. So perhaps rank-and-file believers can take comfort in knowing that even a pastor and biblical scholar can find himself wrestling with doubts. Some uncertainties came from unexpected quarters. Among them was his interest in astronomy, which made him keenly aware of the recently discovered and near-unimaginable scope of the universe with its billions of galaxies.

Dr. Madison found it difficult to reconcile the fact that our planet, the center stage of God's Creation according to Christian theology, was actually one of billions. And rather than being the central hub around which everything in the cosmos revolves, ours is no more than just another of the smaller planets of an ordinary star, lost in a remote arm of a spiral galaxy—itself pinwheeling in its local neighborhood of a still greater galactic conglomeration, in an incomprehensibly vast universe.

But the challenges to his faith weren't all external. Even his high-level doctrinal training for ministry proved to be fraught with problems. The more he advanced in seminary study, the more the cracks in Christian thought showed.

This brief recap is making a long story very short. In a nutshell, these and still other pressures continued to build until, after years of devoted Bible study and service as a trained minister, by the time David had finished his Ph.D. in Biblical studies, he decided it was time to leave and walked away from the faith. *He had studied his way out of Christianity.*

For Christian readers, at this point, it seems like a fair warning is in order. If you are harboring doubts about your faith, this book might add to them. You will see there really are things you wish Jesus hadn't taught and that there are even major obstacles to actually knowing what Jesus taught. As the saying goes, this book is for mature audiences only.

David Fitzgerald

www.centerforinquiry.org/speakers/fitzgerald_david/

Table of Contents

Introduction

Devout followers of Jesus pay special attention to his words, and many love a special edition of the Bible in which the words of Jesus are printed in red. Bible editors use this technique to reinforce confidence that Jesus actually spoke the words—and it works. "I know what Jesus said in the Bible, because it's written in red," said one woman to her new pastor.[1]

When I was a kid growing up in a conservative Methodist Church in rural Indiana, some of these words in red didn't sound quite right to me. For example, to one man who wanted to follow Jesus but said he had to go bury his father first, Jesus replied, "Let the dead bury their own dead, but as for you, go and proclaim the kingdom of God."[2] That seemed rude to me, but Jesus was our Lord and Savior, so I couldn't let it bother me too much. But the problem of questionable Jesus sayings didn't go away. In fact, it got worse the more I read the gospels carefully as I got older.

In *Part 1: Ten Troublesome Teachings,* I'll direct your attention to ten Jesus teachings that are far more

---

[1] Daniel Dennett and Linda LaScola, *Caught in the Pulpit: Leaving Belief Behind*, (Durham: Pitchstone Publishing, Expanded and Updated Edition, 2015), p. 29.
[2] Luke 9:60, NRSV.

troublesome than his one-off comment about burying the dead. Even if you attend church regularly, it's possible you might not have noticed these teachings—or you've noticed, but it makes you too uncomfortable to dwell on them.

The obvious question here is: How could I be so presumptuous that I would claim to know that Christians wish Jesus hadn't taught certain things, and if so, what those things might be. It's a fair question. The answer is simple.

> **When large numbers—perhaps the majority of Christians—ignore a teaching of Jesus or insist that its meaning is something dramatically different from what his words clearly communicate, it is logical to assume these Christians would be more comfortable if Jesus had never said such a thing.**

I'm calling out a silent rebellion by followers of Jesus—including many of his most devout disciples—against some of his key teachings. One characteristic of these teachings is that if they were uttered by anyone other than Jesus, these same believers would reject them immediately and openly instead of pretending they must mean something else or are too mysterious to grasp.

As my ideas for this book were coming together, I reread the gospels carefully—for the umpteenth time in my 78 years—and this time built a chart listing the problematic

Jesus sayings in the gospels. In making this list, I went along with the common Christian assumption that the gospel authors captured the real words of Jesus—that we can pick up the Bible and find out what Jesus really said—an assumption that makes all these words fair game for careful and critical scrutiny.

Just how did I determine which sayings belonged on the chart? I had a few standards in mind. One was moral value. Another was distance from magical thinking and superstition. But another issue guided me as well—a bit of wisdom from my childhood. In attorney Joseph N. Welch's famous 1954 encounter with Senator Joseph McCarthy—now so long ago and far away—Welch asked him: "Have you no sense of decency, sir? At long last, have you no sense of decency?" I was looking for decency in Jesus. When I came across sayings that failed the decency test, I added them to the list.

The total count of problematic quotes by Jesus came to 292. But I didn't want my readers to get bogged down in an endless discussion of them all, so I decided to focus on ten teachings of Jesus that Christians themselves appear to agree are problematic.[3]

Each of the ten chapters in *Part 1* summarizes commands, warnings, or promises taught by Jesus that Christians

---

[3] On this book's website, www.BadThingsJesusTaught.com, you will find a chart listing all 292 of these Jesus quotes, grouped into four categories: scary extremism, preaching about the end time, bad advice and bad theology, and the unreal Jesus in John's gospel.

appear to wish he had never said. In some cases, the embarrassing statement is recorded only one time in the gospels. In other instances, Jesus is reported to have said much the same thing on more than one occasion or in more than one way.

In each of these chapters, I'll explain what's bad about the teaching, and I'll point to evidence that it's a teaching that makes Christians squirm.

Facing up to the problematic Jesus teachings instead of ignoring or reframing them makes it hard for even an earnest Christian to hold on to the idealized, perfect version of Jesus portrayed by priests and preachers for centuries. If, after reading the first ten chapters, you find yourself distressed by the questionable Jesus teachings highlighted there, in *Chapter 11: Four Obstacles to Knowing What Jesus Said*, you will find there is a way out, but one that may hold little appeal: Maybe Jesus didn't say all those upsetting things.

That's the question, "Did Jesus really say all those words in red?" Are some of Jesus' troublesome teachings not actually *his*?

It's no secret that even devout New Testament scholars are justifiably skeptical about so much that we find in the gospels. In *Chapter 11* we'll look at why scholars have reason to suspect misattribution. We'll examine four obstacles that stand between us and the *real* words of Jesus.

If we can't rely on all the content of the gospels, can we rely on the portrait of Jesus we find in the last and most compelling gospel as far as the deity of Jesus is concerned? In *Chapter 12: Two Versions of Jesus*, we will see that the author of John's gospel wanted to distance himself from the other gospel writers. He had a different story to tell. But was he right?

Christians have always been confident that it's important to share the message of the gospels. After all, before ascending into heaven, Jesus commanded his followers:

> **Go therefore and make disciples of all nations, baptizing them in the name of the Father and of the Son and of the Holy Spirit, and teaching them to obey everything that I have commanded you. (Matthew 28:19-20, NRSV)**

Disciples are learners, and one could say that the job of Christian disciples is to learn and to obey the teachings of Jesus and to persuade others—all over the world—to do so as well. But "obey *everything* I have commanded you" isn't so easy if you feel a need to ignore or reinterpret many of the key teachings of Jesus. And there's added confusion if we can't be sure which gospel portrait of Jesus is accurate.

If you are a Christian, I challenge you to be honest with yourself as you read this book. You may find it tempting to look the other way or to go into biblical interpretation autopilot—viewing these Jesus statements as you've long been taught to see them by your religious teachers, assuming that everything in the gospels is reliable and true, and believing that there's only one version of Jesus portrayed in the gospels. But I'm urging you to look again carefully, to try to grasp how these things would sound to you if you heard or read them for the first time today without having a predetermined belief that the person who said them was God walking the earth as a man. I'm urging you to take a hard, honest look at the true nature of the gospel writings, and I'm asking you to be open to the possibility that the nature and identity of Jesus in Christian thinking evolved over the decades during which the four gospels were written.

David Madison

Part 1 - Ten Troublesome Teachings

1 - Be Careful Not to Love Too Much

One of the first things children learn in Sunday School is "God is love." And adult Christians understand that Jesus taught us to love God with all our hearts and to love our neighbors as we love ourselves.[4]

Even if you are not a follower of Jesus, you likely understand that Christianity places a major emphasis on love—the love that comes from God, the love we are called to give back to him, and the love we are to display toward other people. So, why would I begin my list of things Christians wish Jesus hadn't taught with what could be labeled as an outrageous assertion—that *Jesus warned his followers not to love too much*?

The answer is simple: Although Jesus is not reported to have spoken these exact words—be careful not to love too much—they are a toned-down paraphrase of what he taught on more than one occasion and in more ways than

---

[4] See Matthew 22:37-39.

one. Here's an example:

> **Whoever comes to me and does not hate father and mother, wife and children, brothers and sisters, yes, and even life itself, cannot be my disciple. (Luke 14:26, NRSV)**

What a shock, right? There are three typical reactions to this verse. One is to ignore it. Another is to explain it away—to reinterpret its meaning so radically that the "correct understanding" of the passage moves astonishingly far away from the offensive nature of Jesus' recorded words. Still another reaction may occur: Denial.

I once fell into casual conversation with a devout Catholic woman as she went on and on about her beautiful church and her glorious Lord Jesus. I asked her how she felt about the verse referenced above, Luke 14:26, which I quoted to her. She became very angry. She was sure I was lying and blurted out, "There could be no such verse!" She had never heard this verse from the pulpit, and she had not come across it in her own reading of the Bible.

She adored the version of Jesus presented by her priests but was offended when I quoted words of Jesus included in her own New Testament.

I understand that it's frightening to have your faith challenged when it means everything to you. But I also believe that if one's faith is strong, it should be able to stand up to sincere questioning, especially when the question is simply, "What do you think these words of Jesus mean?"

Actually, we can see explaining away an obvious but unpleasant teaching of Jesus as another form of denial Here's what *explaining away* looks like: "Jesus didn't mean that—he couldn't have." Translation: ***The meaning of anything Jesus said has to sync with the version of Jesus I've been taught through the years****. And in this case, Jesus simply could not have meant "hate". He was using a style of speaking, a form of overemphasis or exaggeration to get his point across.*

But we cannot evade the clear meaning of the New Testament Greek, and the word for hate, *miseo*, is used in this text. Hector Avalos has done a splendid analysis of Luke 14:26 in his book, *The Bad Jesus*. The book includes a 39-page chapter on this verse with a simple bottom line: The verse means what it appears to mean.[5]

If your objection is that Jesus would not have taught that we should hate family members, then you must explain why Luke *reported* that Jesus said it. Earlier in Luke 14, Jesus says: "But when you give a banquet, invite the poor, the crippled, the lame, and the blind. And you will be blessed, because they cannot repay you, for you will be repaid at the resurrection of the righteous."[6] Jesus then

---

[5] Hector Avalos, *The Bad Jesus: The Ethics of New Testament Ethics*, (Sheffield: Sheffield Phoenix Press Ltd, 2015), pp. 50-89.
[6] Luke 14:13-14, NRSV.

shares the Parable of the Great Banquet. In the parable, the invited guests—friends of the well-to-do host—all decline at the last minute, but the host is undeterred:

> Then the owner of the house became angry and said to his slave, "Go out at once into the streets and lanes of the town and bring in the poor, the crippled, the blind, and the lame." And the slave said, "Sir, what you ordered has been done, and there is still room." Then the master said to the slave, "Go out into the roads and lanes, and compel people to come in, so that my house may be filled. For I tell you, none of those who were invited will taste my dinner." (Luke 14:21-24, NRSV)

The key message of this parable is that all kinds of people will be welcome in the coming kingdom of Jesus, but there's also a warning to those who turn down the invite. And this "inclusive" parable is followed by a stern warning that appears to be carefully placed and highly intentional, the verse cited at the beginning of this chapter.

> **Whoever comes to me and does not hate father and mother, wife and children, brothers and sisters, yes, and even life itself, cannot be my disciple. (Luke 14:26, NRSV)**

Jesus—in the script included by Luke—issues a strong caution, which amounts to: "You are welcome, no matter what your status, but we don't want anyone with divided loyalties. Family no longer matters as much as our network of fellow believers."

Hector Avalos is blunt:

> How would we judge a modern religious leader who said that we should prefer him over our families? Why would we not treat such a person as an egomaniacal cult leader who does what all cult leaders do: transfer allegiance from one's family to him or her. In other words, the demand would be viewed as unethical in itself.[7]

The need to explain away difficult sayings by Jesus is not limited to rank and file believers. Some Bible translators conspire to tone down the hate-your-family verse. For example, *The Message Bible* presents this rewording: "Anyone who comes to me but refuses to let go of father, mother, spouse, children, brothers, sisters—yes, even one's own self!—can't be my disciple."[8] But does this rendering remove any discomfort one might have with what Jesus said? Is "letting go of family" that much easier to take than "hating one's family"? And shouldn't it trouble us that this interpretation requires that translators obscure the meaning of the original Greek—in other words, that they lie? But disliking something Jesus said is hard to admit when you're a committed believer, and a common response would be: "Surely what Jesus said must

---

[7] Hector Avalos, *The Bad Jesus*, p. 89.

[8] *The Message: The Bible in Contemporary Language*, Luke 14:26, no date, https://messagebible.com/scripture/?text=Luke+14%3A26.

mean something that is good for us. We just need to find the right understanding of what he really meant."

If that's how you feel, you might find some temporary comfort in Matthew's rendering of Jesus' words: "Whoever loves father or mother more than me is not worthy of me; and whoever loves son or daughter more than me is not worthy of me."[9] This is certainly less troubling than the call to hate members of one's family, but the question is: *How many Christians even try to obey either version of Jesus' words on this subject?*

Perhaps the best reason to believe that Christians wish Jesus hadn't uttered either Matthew or Luke's version of this teaching is that virtually no one in the Christian community practices it. And that's not surprising. How do you love an invisible, silent God more than, for example, your newborn son or daughter?

Another reason to acknowledge that Jesus taught his followers to *be careful not to love too much* is found in Luke's gospel, a text I mentioned in the Introduction. Jesus asked a man to follow him, but the fellow said,

> **"Lord, first let me go and bury my father." But Jesus said to him, "Let the dead bury their own dead; but as for you, go and proclaim the kingdom of God." Another said, "I will follow you, Lord; but let me first say farewell to those**

---

[9] Matthew 10:37, NRSV.

> **at my home." Jesus said to him, "No one who puts a hand to the plow and looks back is fit for the kingdom of God." (Luke 9:59-62, NRSV)**

Even as a child, something about this passage bothered me. Can you imagine telling the leader of any organization that you wanted to join, that you were excited about becoming a member, but your father just died, and you would be joining the leader's group after attending your father's funeral, then being told, "Let the dead bury their own dead"? I can't imagine still joining that group!

And it looks like Jesus practiced what he preached about not loving family too much. On one occasion, his mother and his brothers came to him, but they could not reach him because of the crowd surrounding him.

> **"Your mother and your brothers are standing outside, wanting to see you." But he said to them, "My mother and my brothers are those who hear the word of God and do it." (Luke 8:20-21, NRSV)**

This has to be a confusing response for believers who constantly champion the cause of family values!

Jesus taught that we should love our neighbors as ourselves. We should be like the Good Samaritan and help a stranger in trouble. We should turn the other cheek and love our enemies. But we need to be careful about loving our families too much? Honestly, doesn't that bother you?

The modern 12-Step Recovery movement has made us aware of the concept of codependency—the idea that you may habitually "love" other people in a way that consistently harms you. But the goal of recovery from codependency is not to stop loving. It's about learning to love with appropriate boundaries.

Jesus is saying something different. His concern seems to be getting his followers to disconnect from those closest to them. Loving strangers and Samaritans is okay. But loving your family too much is another matter. Jesus almost sounds jealous of the close relationships in a believer's life.

For me, the Luke 14:26 passage cited first in this chapter is unsettling on still another level.

> **Whoever comes to me and does not hate father and mother, wife and children, brothers and sisters, yes, and even life itself, cannot be my disciple. (Luke 14:26, NRSV)**

Hatred of father and mother, wife and children, brothers and sisters is bad enough, but then this: loyalty to Jesus requires *hatred of life itself.* Are you comfortable with this mandate for how you should view life?

A short time ago, a devout man I know, who was about to retire, was distraught when a middle-aged friend of his dropped dead. His friend was out on routine errands when he collapsed and died. And what was the response of my devout acquaintance? He decided to travel as much as possible, to see the world and savor what life has to offer. There's no doubt he still loves Jesus, but he has no interest in "hating life" as a part of his Christian commitment.

We notice immediately when a modern cult takes hating life to the extreme. In November 1978, 900 people committed mass suicide. They drank the Kool-Aid—literally. Their actions were choreographed by the People's Temple cult leader, Jim Jones. Such events prompt immediate revulsion. Most people—including the most devout Christians—quickly and clearly distance themselves from such behavior. But when it's something Jesus said a long time ago, that's different.

Here's one more way in which Jesus warned his followers against loving too much. As he sends his disciples out to share his message, he communicates—in effect—that they should reject anyone who rejects him.

> **If anyone will not welcome you or listen to your words, shake off the dust from your feet as you leave that house or town. Truly I tell you, it will be more tolerable for the land of Sodom and Gomorrah on the day of judgment than for that town. (Matthew 10:14-15, NRSV)**

When you've been a believer for most of your life, it's easy to overlook how extreme this is.

Sodom and Gomorrah were burned to the ground. So, any

town that ignores wandering itinerate preachers faces the same fate? Try to imagine yourself in a similar situation. What happens when Mormon missionaries or Jehovah's Witnesses knock on your door? Most of us send them on their way. We can't be bothered. How would you react if one of them turned and yelled at you as they walked away, "Just you wait, God will burn your house down!" There's no other way to see this teaching as anything but brutal and chilling.

Shaking the dust off one's feet is a symbolic way of saying, "I want nothing more to do with you." Ask any formerly sincere Christian who has left the faith if they understand such shunning. I can assure you the answer will be *Yes*.

If you are a follower of Jesus and wish he hadn't warned his followers to be careful not to love too much, I can understand why.

2 - Don't Worry about Basic Human Needs

Jesus taught his followers to recognize the transitory nature of this life. He spoke in the imperative when he warned his followers about accumulating earthly treasures. Instead, he said, they should aim to store up treasures in heaven.

> **Do not store up for yourselves treasures on earth, where moth and rust consume and where thieves break in and steal; but store up for yourselves treasures in heaven, where neither moth nor rust consumes and where thieves do not break in and steal. For where your treasure is, there your heart will be also. (Matthew 6:19-21, NRSV)**

"Do not store up treasures" might have made sense to Jesus as an ancient preacher who was sure all earthly regimes and practices were about to be eliminated with the anticipated arrival of the Kingdom of God. But that didn't happen, and the verses cited in this chapter are still in the New Testament.

A handful of Christians do indeed retreat to monastic life, shunning earthly possessions and devoting themselves to keeping their focus on God and his kingdom.

But most Christians probably wish Jesus had never said such things. Apparently, followers of Jesus want nice houses and cars as much as anyone else. If they have the money, they accumulate flat-screen TVs, jewelry, decorative items, gadgets, and a host of other "indispensable" consumer products. Just look at a wish list on a bridal registry for a Christian couple. The primary response to this teaching by most Christians—at least in developed countries—is to simply pretend Jesus never taught such things.

A few verses after the passage quoted above, Jesus becomes even more extreme when he teaches that God ("your heavenly Father") knows what you need, and if you put his kingdom first, this heavenly father will provide your food and clothing.

> **...do not worry about your life, what you will eat or what you will drink, or about your body, what you will wear. Is not life more than food, and the body more than clothing? Look at the birds of the air; they neither sow nor reap nor gather into barns, and yet your heavenly Father feeds them. (Matthew 6:25-26, NRSV)**
>
> **Therefore do not worry, saying, 'What will we eat?' or 'What will we drink?' or 'What will we**

> **wear?' For it is the Gentiles who strive for all these things; and indeed your heavenly Father knows that you need all these things. But strive first for the kingdom of God and his righteousness, and all these things will be given to you as well. (Matthew 6:31-33, NRSV)**

It has long been recognized that the author of the Gospel of Matthew represented a faction of the early Jesus sect more sympathetic to its Jewish heritage, perhaps in resistance to Paul's message of Gentile inclusion. Even so, it is a bit jarring to find Jesus ridiculing the Gentiles for being concerned about what to eat, drink, and wear. This seems to be bragging: "We can do better because we are better." But then comes an absurd promise: food, drink, and clothing will be given to those who "strive first for the kingdom." This sounds like an invitation to plunge into fantasies about how life works.

If you insist these words of Jesus from Matthew 6 accurately describe how the world works, then I must assume that showing up for work is not a priority for you and that you don't believe in insurance, savings accounts, or planning for retirement. And I must also assume that your priority every day is putting God's kingdom first—making it more important than your own physical needs, your own family, and your personal future on this earth.

There has never been a time in human history when people have been free from the hard labor of making sure there is enough to eat. In fact, God himself made sure this is the case, according to Genesis 3:17-19 (NRSV), with his curse on Adam:

> ...cursed is the ground because of you; in toil you shall eat of it all the days of your life; thorns and thistles it shall bring forth for you; and you shall eat the plants of the field. By the sweat of your face you shall eat bread until you return to the ground, for out of it you were taken; you are dust, and to dust you shall return.

And I could name many examples of cases in which "the Father" fails to feed people:

> Only a thin lifeline of supplies could be brought in to Leningrad's three million residents on the 'Road of Life,' which crossed the frozen waters of Lake Ladoga. It could not save them all; in December 1941 alone more than fifty thousand died of starvation.[10]

Wasn't God up to this task? Were none of the 50,000 who died seeking his kingdom above all else? And if that were the case—that no one qualified in the putting-kingdom-first category—then the standard must be too hard for

---

[10] Lynn H. Nicholas, *The Rape of Europa: The Fate of Europe's Treasures in the Third Reich and the Second World War*, (New York: Vintage Books, 1995), p. 196

anyone to attain.

In Matthew and Mark, we read about the miraculous feeding of 4,000 with just a few loaves and fishes, and all four gospels report that the same deed was also done for 5,000. Such tales make Jesus and God look good, but the experience of Leningrad puts the lie to these gospel fantasies.

Jesus taught his followers to be encouraged by how God "clothes" the lilies of the field.

> **And why do you worry about clothing? Consider the lilies of the field, how they grow; they neither toil nor spin, yet I tell you, even Solomon in all his glory was not clothed like one of these. But if God so clothes the grass of the field, which is alive today and tomorrow is thrown into the oven, will he not much more clothe you—you of little faith? (Matthew 6:28-30, NRSV)**

Again, this is not the way the world works, and even the most devout followers of Jesus know it. The Christians I know worry about clothes, not just having clothes to wear, but in the sense of being fashion conscious. They pay no attention to Jesus whatever on this. We can be sure that the couture specialists at the Vatican—its costume budget every year could feed thousands—ignore this advice as well. Notice the dig at the end of the passage: anyone who does worry about clothing is ridiculed for lack of faith.

How do we know when Christians wish Jesus hadn't said something? They ignore it or explain it away. As mentioned above, ignoring appears to be the favorite response to this teaching, but here's what the explain-it-away approach looks like—although this seems like guesswork, pretending to read Jesus' mind:

> Obviously, Jesus didn't mean we weren't supposed to work for a living, and he certainly didn't mean we shouldn't save for a rainy day or insure ourselves against what might happen. What he meant was for us to be responsible in these ways while always remembering it's up to him to make sure these things work—to make sure we have a job, to make sure that we don't find ourselves without the basic things we need despite our attempts to plan and be responsible.

This sounds a lot like the non-biblical but oft-quoted statement, "God takes care of those who take care of themselves," and not much at all like these Jesus sayings in Matthew 6, that his followers should not worry about their basic human needs.

3 - Never Say No to a Borrower

Just in case you still don't think Jesus taught his followers to be financially irresponsible, here's another thing Christians certainly wish he hadn't said.

> **...do not refuse anyone who wants to borrow from you. (Matthew 5:42, NRSV)**

How do we know Christians wish Jesus had not spoken these words? We know because they ignore this imperative, or at best, they infrequently practice what it teaches.

Do you know anyone—Christian or not—who always says *Yes* when anyone asks them for a loan? I don't.

I know of only one possible exception. Parents can fall into the trap of bailing an irresponsible son or daughter out of financial dilemmas over and over. But any impartial observer knows such behavior is a flaw, not a virtue.

I may be uninformed, but have any Christians created any banks that always say Yes to loan applications?

And believers need to be careful with this guideline because it seems to contradict another: If you say *Yes* to a would-be borrower who is a family member, you may be disobeying the *be careful not to love too much* guideline. It's a conundrum. If you say *No* to the would-be borrower's request, you will be a disobedient follower. But if you say *Yes* to a family member's loan request, you may be guilty of loving family more than Jesus wants you to.

The simple truth is that always saying *Yes* when anyone asks to borrow money is awful advice that could easily lead to one's own financial ruin. But that's not the only bad advice found in Matthew 5. Here's the don't-say-no-to-a-borrower verse along with the verses preceding it.

> **You have heard that it was said, 'An eye for an eye and a tooth for a tooth.' But I say to you, 'Do not resist an evildoer. But if anyone strikes you on the right cheek, turn the other also; and if anyone wants to sue you and take your coat, give your cloak as well; and if anyone forces you to go one mile, go also the second mile. Give to everyone who begs from you, and do not refuse anyone who wants to borrow from you. (Matthew 5:38-42, NRSV)**

This is a cluster of bad guidance. A massive amount of human misery could be avoided if human disputes could be settled without retaliation—as in eye-for-eye and tooth-for-tooth. But Jesus offers no realistic alternative here. If taken seriously, "Do not resist an evildoer" would plunge society into chaos. We take it for granted that evil and evildoers must be resisted. Martin Luther King adopted non-violent, turn-the-other-cheek resistance as a tactic, but he was committed to resisting evil and evildoers.

I'll give Jesus an out here: We can understand his do-not-resist-evil advice when we see him as an apocalyptic prophet who believed the kingdom of God would arrive on earth—eliminating all evildoers—within the lifetime of his listeners. But that didn't happen!

What did occur? During two millennia human society has survived, improved, and advanced to the extent that evil and evildoers have been resisted vigorously.

And what about the other teachings in the passage cited above? If you're a Christian, this might be a good time to ask yourself if you honestly believe the following imperatives:

- If anyone forces you to go one mile, go also the second mile.
- If anyone wants to sue you and take your coat, give your cloak as well.
- Give to everyone who begs from you.

"Go the extra mile" has become a cliché for putting out extra effort, without embracing the element of coercion that was present in the life of Jesus' listeners when a Roman soldier exercised his right to force someone to carry his pack for one mile. As for the guidelines about responding to lawsuits and beggars, even the most devout believers would have to admit this is not how they respond to the world.

It makes sense for a great moral teacher to urge followers to be empathetic and generous, and it could be argued that is what Jesus had in mind. But the impracticality of his teachings here detracts from that message.

There's still more confusing advice in Matthew's chapter 5.

> **But I say to you, love your enemies and pray for those who persecute you, so that you may be children of your Father in heaven; for he makes his sun rise on the evil and on the good, and sends rain on the righteous and on the unrighteous. For if you love those who love you, what reward do you have? Do not even the tax collectors do the same? And if you greet only your brothers, what more are you doing than others? (Matthew 5:44-47, NRSV)**

If you believe in prayer, praying for those who make your life difficult sounds like a good and charitable thing to do. But "love your enemies" sounds strange coming from the holy hero who downgraded love for one's family. As we have seen, in Luke 14: 26, Jesus stipulates hatred of family as a condition for being a disciple—a deliberate attempt to intensify Matthew's suggestion that followers had to love

Jesus more than family members. How is loving enemies supposed to make sense in the context of his teaching that his followers should *be careful not to love too much*?

The most pressing question here is: Does God the Father love *his* enemies? In the Old Testament, he is known as Yahweh—a raging tribal deity—and is not much improved in the New Testament: Jesus speaks of fiery hell and suffering worse than at the time of Noah when the Kingdom arrives. The idea that God loves his enemies is a pretty hard sell.[11]

Going beyond the I'll-watch-your-back-if-you-watch-my-back standard for altruism and being more loving than the next person is a noble goal. But does it trouble you that Jesus is teaching his followers to base their choices about how to love on what reward they will receive? Wouldn't it be better to be a loving person just because that's who you are? Wouldn't it be better to be generous with others just because that's how you choose to live?

It's embarrassing to need to correct the man so many humans regard as the world's greatest teacher, but this bad advice in the Sermon on the Mount is disappointing. We all know that relating to others requires boundaries, but Jesus doesn't seem to grasp that boundaries are destroyed

---

[11] See especially Dan Barker, *God the Most Unpleasant Character in All Fiction* and Steve Wells, *Drunk with Blood: God's Killings in the Bible*.

if we're supposed to always give to beggars, always say Yes to people who ask for loans, and always give more than we're asked for.

And there are different kinds of enemies. Some can be won over. Others cannot. The command to "love our enemies" plays into the hands of sociopaths, who would love for you to follow all these teachings. The message they would see from such behavior on your part would be: You can use this person without any pushback. To put it another way, Jesus seems to be teaching his followers to go on autopilot and respond passively to hostile, even evil, actions by others who will simply see such a response as permission for continued manipulation, boundary-violating, and abuse.

There's plenty of bad advice here—advice that is consistently ignored or explained away by the followers of Jesus. But the most transparent response by Christians, the clearest indicator that they wish Jesus hadn't taught such things, can be seen in their failure to *never say no to a borrower.*

4 - Give Me Everything

How committed should a follower of Jesus be? The answer is: Totally committed! Christians used to sing a hymn that asks, "Is your all on the altar?" When it comes to commitment to Jesus, the operative word is ALL.

> **...you shall love the Lord your God with all your heart, and with all your soul, and with all your mind, and with all your strength. (Mark 12:30, NRSV)**

There are Christians who withdraw to monasteries and convents to try to achieve this ***all, all, all, all*** level of commitment, but most Christians have their lives to lead. They have their jobs, families, hobbies, vacations—and make no pretense of giving ***all***.

If you're a follower of Jesus, ponder the implications of this text for your own life. Is it even possible to give God all? And why does the powerful God who is described as self-sufficient require this level of commitment—a level that few, if any, believers even strive for, let alone attain.

There is a narrative version of this ***all, all, all, all*** demand.

In the book of Acts, we read that "…the whole group of those who believed were of one heart and soul, and no one claimed private ownership of any possessions, but everything they owned was held in common."[12] In this context, those who owned houses or property sold them and gave the proceeds to the church. But a couple named Ananias and Sapphira sold a piece of property, and when they made their donation, they lied about how much they had gotten for the property, holding back some of the money for themselves. Peter scolded Ananias severely for lying and withholding whereupon he dropped dead and was buried right away. A few hours later, Peter gave the same scolding to Sapphira, and she dropped dead too. The result: "And great fear seized the whole church and all who heard of these things."[13] Is that any way to run a church?

I'm guessing that few Christians read this story and say, "Wow, that's cool. I need to step up my game!" Instead, the norm is to ignore the incident or explain it away: That was then. This is now.

Sometimes the need to give ***All*** is more subtly stated. At the end of Mark 12, we find Jesus watching people making their contributions in the Temple. He wasn't impressed with rich people putting in lots of cash, but a widow was worthy of comment for putting in "two small copper coins worth a penny."

---

[12] Acts 4:32 NRSV.

[13] Acts 5:11, NRSV.

> **Truly I tell you, this poor widow has put in more than all those who are contributing to the treasury. For all of them have contributed out of their abundance; but she out of her poverty has put in everything she had, all she had to live on. (Mark 12:43-44, NRSV)**

This script fits Mark's theme about extreme commitment earlier in the same chapter, and religious bureaucrats have commonly championed "giving until it hurts." Yes, it's a legitimate point that the rich don't deserve high praise for giving away what they won't miss, but commending the poor widow for her deed? That's another matter.

Under any normal, rational idea of what makes sense, it was not smart that the widow "put in all she had to live on." It's more logical to wonder why Jesus didn't help her get the money back. Why would Jesus commend a mindset that prompts a widow to give away—to a mammoth religious bureaucracy—all the money she has to live on?

In case it's still not clear that Jesus wants everything from his followers, consider this text:

> **Then he said to them all, "If any want to become my followers, let them deny themselves and take up their cross daily and follow me. For those who want to save their life will lose it, and those who lose their life for my sake will save it. What does it profit them if they gain the whole world, but lose or forfeit themselves? Those**

> **who are ashamed of me and of my words, of them the Son of Man will be ashamed when he comes in his glory and the glory of the Father and of the holy angels." (Luke 9:23-26, NRSV)**

These orders from Jesus would immediately be labeled as extremist and cultish if uttered by any new-on-the-scene contemporary religious leader. Deny yourself. Lose your life for my sake. And it's not enough to practice these things—you must never be ashamed of these teachings, even if part of you realizes how unreasonable they are.

Such imperatives go against normal cognitive functioning. We have evolved to survive. Altruism—sharing and working together—is a part of that survival mentality, but survival also means taking care of yourself.

If you are a Christian, I'm sure you've heard countless times the virtues of "taking up your cross and following Jesus." My question for you is, what does taking up your cross actually mean in your daily life? How do you practically obey the command of Jesus to lose your life? And to what extent are you denying yourself on a daily basis? It's possible that you've developed some sophisticated, work-around answers to these questions that make sense to you. But here's a teaching that's much more difficult to explain away:

> **So therefore, none of you can become my disciple if you do not give up all your possessions. (Luke 14:33 NRSV)**

Certainly this teaching has not stood the test of time. Even the most faithful believers pay little or no attention to it—sure evidence that Christians wish Jesus hadn't said it.

I guess there's always a life preserver for such difficult verses. In this case, you might hopefully raise the possibility that this teaching applied only to the original disciples. If you're on the ground with Jesus looking for the Kingdom of God to descend on earth in the near future, why would you need your possessions? But the problem—once again—is that the kingdom Jesus predicted did not appear within the lifetime of any of his listeners (and *still* hasn't appeared!), so this isn't a life preserver after all.

This expectation of the imminent return of Jesus shows itself in other ways as well. There is no hint in the New Testament that its authors treasured so many things that humans have accomplished. They offer no praise for literature, philosophy, architecture, painting, or sculpture— in other words, for so many of the splendid accomplishments of the ancient world.

Today, many devout Christians do value such things, apparently ignoring the promise of Jesus that he could return at any time and the imperative to rid oneself of all possessions. The only way to understand some of the promises Jesus made is to realize they made sense only if he did return within the lifetimes of his listeners.

And how do we wrap our minds around this next troublesome teaching?

> **Truly I tell you, there is no one who has left house or brothers or sisters or mother or father or children or fields, for my sake and for the sake of the good news, who will not receive a hundredfold now in this age—houses, brothers and sisters, mothers and children, and fields, with persecutions—and in the age to come eternal life. (Mark 10:29-30, NRSV)**

We can't test the promise of eternal life since none of us reading this book have died, but we know that the hundredfold reimbursement in this life makes no sense whatever. I guess televangelists with private jets can make a case that the hundredfold reward Jesus promised in this life works for them, but their jets were paid for by sacrificial gifts from their sheep-like followers, not by Jesus.

If you're a Christian, I ask you to consider why this Jesus saying isn't a deal-breaker. How can leaving your property and family to follow Jesus—supposedly to gain eternal life—be a way to build a better world?[14]

---

[14] Surely Christians must lament the chaos in the New Testament about how to win eternal life. This statement in Mark is nonsense, of course; in John's gospel we'll see that believing in Jesus is the key—and eating his flesh and drinking his blood. Paul states in Romans 10:9, "...if you confess with your lips that Jesus is Lord and believe in your heart that God raised him from the dead, you will be saved." (NRSV)

These verses make it clear that half-hearted obedience to Jesus is not okay. But since so few Christians come close to giving what anyone could reasonably consider ***all***, shouldn't these requirements be reasons to ask if the Jesus plan really works?

Notice anything about the four chapters you've just read in this book? Each points to something Jesus taught that hardly any Christians actually do.

5 - Remarrying After Divorce Is Adultery

As I pointed out in the Introduction, there are many Jesus sayings that Christians wouldn't take seriously at all if it they didn't know Jesus said them. In this chapter, I'll focus on one of the worst pieces of advice that Jesus ever gave. Here's the preamble:

> Have you not read that the one who made them at the beginning "made them male and female," and said, "For this reason a man shall leave his father and mother and be joined to his wife, and the two shall become one flesh. So they are no longer two, but one flesh." (Matthew 19:4-6a, NRSV)

If you believe that God established the order of creation, then the male-female setup makes good sense. The two join together and become one flesh. So far, so good, but then, few sayings of Jesus have caused more damage than this one:

> **Therefore what God has joined together, let no one separate. (Matthew 19:6b, NRSV)**

Wait a minute: Yes, God arranged the basic setup—men connecting with women—but then he's had his hand in every single marriage? Since humans first began to get married, all these connections have been arranged by God? How can that make sense?

In every aspect of life, people make mistakes, and that includes marrying the wrong person for wrong reasons. But never mind: God participated in the error, he okayed it? Has he signed off on millions of bad marriages? Was he responsible for each specific "joining together"? Then Jesus takes things to an even more troubling level.

> **He said to them, "Whoever divorces his wife and marries another commits adultery against her; and if she divorces her husband and marries another, she commits adultery." (Mark 10:11-12, NRSV)**

This means that, according to Jesus, adultery is rampant among Christians, given the number of good believers who have been divorced and remarried. And one must wonder whether these followers of Jesus are admitting, when they get divorced, that God joining them together was *his* mistake?

Please note, by the way, that Matthew, in the Sermon on the Mount, provided this modification to Mark 10:11-12:

> **But I say to you that anyone who divorces his wife, except on the ground of unchastity, causes her to commit adultery; and whoever marries a**

> **divorced woman commits adultery. (Matthew 5:32, NRSV)**

"…except on the ground of unchastity…" Is it possible that even the writer of one of the gospels was embarrassed by something Jesus taught and added a qualifier to tone it down?

I have devoted a chapter to Jesus' teaching on divorce because it is so glaringly bad and deserves prominent mention. But wait, it gets worse, once he mentions one more way to commit adultery without actually engaging in sex outside of marriage:

> **But I say to you that everyone who looks at a woman with lust has already committed adultery with her in his heart. (Matthew 5:28, NRSV)**

So now Jesus is condemning *sexual feelings*, a teaching that ignores how we are built and has led to unnecessary shame and guilt for centuries. The Greek word translated "lust" in the passage could also mean "longing for" or "desiring." Even the most devout Christians can't help noticing when someone comes across to them as "really sexy" and feeling something that is more than simply appreciation. And anyone—Christian or not—who has ever had a partner understands how important sexual feelings can be in creating a mutual attraction between two individuals.

Despite Jesus' teaching about divorce as adultery and his

even more extreme warning that thinking is as bad as doing, the bulk of Christians go right on getting divorces when things don't work out and feeling normal sexual feelings as they go about their lives. Christians don't have to say they wish Jesus hadn't taught these things. Their actions speak louder than words.

6 - You Are Accountable for Every Word

The high expectations of Jesus—for those who follow him—are not limited to divorce, remarriage, adultery, and sexual purity. He makes it clear that we are accountable for every word we speak.

> **I tell you, on the day of judgment you will have to give an account for every careless word you utter; for by your words you will be justified, and by your words you will be condemned. (Matthew 12:36-37, NRSV)**

This is, in fact, a terrifying warning: God is monitoring every word you utter and plans to get even on judgment day. I really do wonder how many Christians take this seriously. Do you live in constant terror of saying the wrong thing, with such horrible consequences?

In Matthew chapter 5, Jesus provides a specific example of something you can say that could send you to hell.

> **I say to you that if you are angry with a brother you will be liable to judgment; and if you insult**

> **a brother you will be liable to the council; and if you say, 'You fool,' you will be liable to the hell of fire. (Matthew 5:22, NRSV)**

Jesus prefaces this by approving of the ancient law against murder, but then places anger and insults in the same category. Devout folks who make their way in the real world can sense how unrealistic this is—we all get angry and flame out—and how it falls short of being good advice. These warnings in Matthew 5 and 12 are characteristic of a North Korean style of totalitarian monotheism: God monitors everything you do.

The word translated "hell" in Matthew 5 is *Gehenna*, which appears to reference a garbage dump that was always on fire and came to symbolize unending punishment. Wouldn't anyone else who warned that you'll get tossed into fire if you call someone a fool be labeled as a scary extremist?

And there's more of this strangeness. If you want to see Christians ignore this next Jesus commandment, go to any U.S. courtroom.

> **I say to you, "Do not swear at all, either by heaven, for it is the throne of God, or by the earth, for it is his footstool, or by Jerusalem, for it is the city of the great King. And do not swear by your head, for you cannot make one hair white or black. Let your word be 'Yes, Yes' or 'No, No'; anything more than this comes from**

the evil one." (Matthew 5:34-37, NRSV)

One positive way to interpret this text could be, "Say what you mean and mean what you say. Just tell the truth all the time." But, come on, isn't the rest of this teaching worth a big yawn? Especially from those who place their hands on the Bible to swear, "So help me God." This is worthless advice anchored to ancient cosmology that views heaven as a throne and the earth as a footstool. And so much trouble has been caused by giving special status to Jerusalem.

A few Christians do refuse to swear on a Bible because of these words spoken by Jesus. At least they're trying to be consistent. But for most believers I know, refusing to swear an oath because Jesus said not to isn't even on their radar.

But there's more wildly bad advice about words—things you have to *be careful not to say.*

> **They love to have the place of honor at banquets and the best seats in the synagogues, and to be greeted with respect in the marketplaces, and to have people call them rabbi. But you are not to be called rabbi, for you have one teacher, and you are all brothers. And call no one your father on earth, for you have one Father—the one in heaven. Nor are you to be called instructors, for you have one instructor, the Messiah. (Matthew 23:6-10, NRSV)**

The context of these verses is Jesus' scathing denunciation of religious bureaucrats, but his coaching goes off the rails when he forbids his followers to use the words "father" and "instructor" with respect to other humans. That advice never caught on. The Catholic Church flaunts it especially. Aren't its priests disciples of Christ?

And the focus on inappropriate words may sometimes be ***who*** you're speaking about and not just ***what*** you say.

> **... people will be forgiven for every sin and blasphemy, but blasphemy against the Spirit will not be forgiven. Whoever speaks a word against the Son of Man will be forgiven, but whoever speaks against the Holy Spirit will not be forgiven, either in this age or in the age to come. (Matthew 12:31-32, NRSV)**

This text pushes us back into the superstitious thinking of the first century when the spirit realm was thought to be swarming with angels and demons[15]—and at the top of this hierarchy was the Holy Spirit, part of God himself. And what is taught in this passage is puzzling: Why is offending this part of the trinity considered such a colossal error, never to be forgiven?

Mark's version of this teaching provides a clue: People had suggested that Jesus himself was possessed by an unclean spirit. Since Jesus was filled with the Holy Spirit, or better

[15] In Mark, chapter 5, Jesus transfers demons into pigs.

still from a trinitarian point of view, was the Holy Spirit, speaking against him was unforgivable.

Then again, maybe not. When Matthew copied and expanded this fragment of Mark's gospel, he added: "Whoever speaks a word against the Son of Man will be forgiven..." So, it's only blasphemy against the Holy Spirit that is an "eternal sin," as Mark puts it.

Please notice that anyone who takes this text seriously has succumbed to belief in magical curses. Saying a blasphemy out loud alters the fate of your soul. That amounts to a magic spell. As ethical thought has matured over time, those who qualify as great moral teachers have given up endorsing magical curses.

Are you still on the fence about the premise of this chapter, that you are accountable for every word you speak? Listen again to Jesus.

> **"I tell you, on the day of judgment you will have to give an account for every careless word you utter; for by your words you will be justified, and by your words you will be condemned." (Matthew 12:36-37, NRSV)**

How do most Christians deal with this clear warning from Jesus? They jump over to Paul's understanding of the Gospel and comfort themselves with the assurance that by accepting Jesus' sacrifice on the cross, all is forgiven. So, despite the stern admonitions about careless words, they're not worried.

But the focus of this chapter—like all the preceding chapters—is on the New Testament record of what Jesus said. And if you're a believer, these teachings by Jesus beg for a thoughtful response on your part.

The texts I've cited in this chapter are especially bothersome because, again, they are an expression of totalitarian monotheism. It's like always having CCTV cameras watching us: God spies on everything we think and say to make sure we get the punishment we deserve. "Well, Jesus was a man of his time," apologists may point out. But the New Testament and Christian theology position Jesus as far more than "a man of his times." Therefore, we have a right to expect more of his teachings since we know that no human can go through life without ever saying something that is later regretted. The requirement that we manage our words perfectly should be deeply troubling to any follower of Jesus.

7 - You Can Do Magic

At the end of Mark's gospel, we find Jesus uttering words that would likely send anyone who spoke the same words today to a psychiatric ward. Or, if spoken by a wild-eyed, semi-sober, down-and-outer on a street corner, we might just roll our eyes and feel sorry for the poor fellow. Here's what Jesus said:

> **And these signs will accompany those who believe: by my name they will cast out demons; they will speak in new tongues; they will pick up snakes in their hands, and if they drink any deadly thing, it will not hurt them; they will lay their hands on the sick, and they will recover. (Mark 16:17-18, NRSV)**

"By using my name" reflects confidence in a magical spell. This is typical of ancient superstitions that place faith in the *power* of a name: Use this special name, and something out-of-the-ordinary will happen. In this case, the promise is that demons will be expelled. "Speaking in tongues" refers to the incomprehensible babble uttered under the "influence of the Holy Spirit." Picking up serpents? This has commonly been understood as handing poisonous snakes—and surviving. The list concludes with drinking poison and experiencing no harm, and finally, Jesus speaks of curing sick people by touching them.

The heavy dose of magical thinking here is bad enough, but this text is problematic on another level. As Jesus offered parting wisdom in this post-resurrection appearance, wouldn't this have been a great time to remind his followers that true belief would make a difference in how they treated others? Perhaps, "These signs will accompany those who believe: They will show superior compassion to those who are suffering, and they will fight for the rights of the oppressed."

But help is on the way. Christians can breathe a sigh of relief knowing that these verses in Mark 16 are part of a fake ending of Mark. That is, manuscript research has shown that Mark 16:8-20 was not part of the original gospel. Person or persons unknown added them later. But this prompts the question: How did fake verses end up in the Bible?

No help is on the way, however—no breathing sighs of relief—when we consider a few verses in John's gospel that are shocking examples of magical thinking.

First, let's talk about communion, the first of two touchy, delicate subjects.

When I was a kid, I looked forward to communion Sunday because it meant the sermon would be shorter! The preacher couldn't talk as long as he usually did because everyone in the congregation would go to the front of the sanctuary to kneel and "take communion." There were little cubes of *Wonder Bread* and tiny glasses of *Welch's 100% Grape Juice*, which symbolized the body and blood of Jesus. This was an aspect of piety that we just took for granted from an early age: eating and drinking the body and blood of Jesus. And during the communion service, we might sing a hymn that repeated the words, "Are you washed in the blood?" multiple times. No one was there to tap me on the shoulder and say, "That's pretty gross, you know." On the other side of town, at the Catholic Church, all this was *not* symbolic. Catholic theology includes the *miracle of the Mass*—which means that the bread and wine become, literally, the body and blood of Jesus. Here's where the magical thinking kicks in, and with Catholics, it's the priests who are performing the magic trick of turning ordinary bread and wine into the body and blood of Jesus. And they take this seriously—if there's any wine left over, the priest must drink it lest there be cold Jesus blood in the parish refrigerator. I suspect the gospel of John is at fault here.

The familiar words we know from Mark's gospel, "this is my body…this is my blood of the new covenant,"[16] are missing from John's account of the Last Supper. Instead, much earlier in the story, in the 6th chapter of John, after Jesus had fed the 5,000, we find these words—and no matter how familiar you may be with communion—how can they not be disturbing?

> **Very truly, I tell you, unless you eat the flesh of the Son of Man and drink his blood, you have no life in you. Those who eat my flesh and drink my blood have eternal life, and I will raise them up on the last day; for my flesh is true food and my blood is true drink. Those who eat my flesh**

---

[16] Mark 14:22-25, NRSV.

> **and drink my blood abide in me, and I in them. Just as the living Father sent me, and I live because of the Father, so whoever eats me will live because of me. (John 6:53-57, NRSV)**

Perhaps, if I had known this text as a kid, right away, I would have agreed that this is gross. But that's only part of the problem. Whether you're Catholic or Protestant, and take these words literally or symbolically, this passage is about magical thinking and magic potions: eat this, drink that, and you'll get to live forever.

If you take communion, is this what you have in mind? Are you comfortable with the magic potion idea that John's gospel promotes? John seems to have borrowed this from magic lore of the ancient world, and scholar Hector Avalos draws our attention to this major embarrassment:

> Christ's sacrifice is premised on the sort of blood-magic inherited from the ancient Near East... Christian apologists might claim that their god has the authority to order sacrifice, but this claim is no more verifiable than that of any other religion that practices human sacrifice.[17]

That's the first touchy, delicate subject: when you take communion: Is it okay that you're expecting magic potions

---

[17] Hector Avalos, in *The Christian Delusion: Why Faith Fails*, edited by John W. Loftus (Amherst: Prometheus Books, 2010), p. 227.

to work?

Now, on to the second uncomfortable subject: the "enchanted" power of prayer. John's gospel is also a promoter of this type of magical thinking.

> **I will do whatever you ask in my name, so that the Father may be glorified in the Son. If in my name you ask me for anything, I will do it. (John 14:13-14, NRSV)**
>
> **Very truly, I tell you, if you ask anything of the Father in my name, he will give it to you. Until now you have not asked for anything in my name. Ask and you will receive, so that your joy may be complete. (John 16:23-24, NRSV)**

I suspect many Christians know these texts are falsified by their own prayer experiences.

I urge you to think long and hard about prayer. How can it *not* be classified as a form of magical thinking? In many cases, even an attempt at conjuring? Folks who pray are usually earnest about it, thinking with all their might about messages they have for God. But how do the thoughts inside our heads—trapped there by our skulls—escape to be perceived by God? There are no known mechanisms by which that would work, just as there are no known ways by which the popular spells in the Harry Potter stories would work. Nobody even tries to explain how the Fairy God Mother in *Cinderella*, waving a wand, changes a pumpkin into a carriage—because that's fantasy. Does prayer amount to waving a wand in our minds? The efficacy of prayer should not be off-limits for legitimate inquiry. Indeed, scientific studies of prayer have not yielded hoped-for results.[18]

Even as toddlers, we're taught to say our prayers. Hence the practice is so ingrained and accepted *as something that works*. But we're never taught to ask the fundamental question: *how* does this work? You may be used to people saying, "God works in mysterious ways," but for folks who are truly curious—and even a little bit skeptical—this is a non-answer.

Two problematic things about prayer must be faced:

1. The concept of prayer brings us face-to-face, again, with the grim specter of totalitarian monotheism, that is to say, God monitors our very thoughts—the ultimate invasion of privacy for every person on earth. Doesn't that make God a nosy busybody? Aside from the fact that there is no verifiable evidence to back up this idea—our *feelings* about prayer instilled since childhood are not the kind of hard evidence required—it's simply a terrible idea.
2. *It is incredibly implausible* that a God who manages the cosmos, that is, who has hundreds of billions of galaxies, and trillions of planets under management, would be interested in monitoring the thoughts of more than seven billion human beings—as a way of keeping track of their sinful inclinations, their need for a parking space, or

[18] *New York Times*, "Long-Awaited Medical Study Questions the Power of Prayer," March 31, 2006, https://www.nytimes.com/2006/03/31/health/longawaited-medical-study-questions-the-power-of-prayer.html.

recovery from an ailment. Such an attentive God might have made sense long ago when the earth was regarded as *the* center of his attention, and when God was thought to reside in the realm above the clouds.

These considerations make it hard to take prayer seriously, and the problem is aggravated when we see that Jesus—a man of the first century—made totally unrealistic promises about prayer, putting it firmly in the realm of magic spells. In addition to the verses in John mentioned above, we find these quotes in Matthew:

> **Again, truly I tell you, if two of you agree on earth about anything you ask, it will be done for you by my Father in heaven. (Matthew 18:19, NRSV)**

> **For truly I tell you, if you have faith the size of a mustard seed, you will say to this mountain, 'Move from here to there,' and it will move; and nothing will be impossible for you. (Matthew 17:20, NRSV)**

Not only will you be able to do magic, but you'll also get whatever you want.

> **Truly I tell you, if you have faith and do not doubt, not only will you do what has been done to the fig tree, but even if you say to this mountain, 'Be lifted up and thrown into the sea,' it will be done. Whatever you ask for in prayer with faith, you will receive. (Matthew**

21:21-22, NRSV)

Yes, we can accept that "move mountains" is hyperbole, a metaphor to make a point. But the promises made here are not reality-based, as even the most devout believers will admit:

- When two agree about what to ask, it will be done for you.
- Nothing will be impossible for you.
- Whatever you ask for in prayer with faith, you will receive.

Christians have organized prayer marathons—far more than two people agree what to ask—to coax God to heal a desperately ill member of the congregation; as often as not, these prayers don't get the job done.

These magical spells and formulas haven't worked.

Guilt can follow in the wake of unanswered prayers. Are you familiar with these mind games to figure out why prayers fail?

- My faith isn't strong enough. It's my fault.
- God works in mysterious ways.
- What I asked for wasn't within his God's will.
- I didn't pray hard enough.
- Maybe, to punish me, God isn't answering my prayers.

Overpromising what prayers can accomplish and hyping the importance of faith as a key ingredient—contribute to the suspicion that this part of religion has been oversold. Cynics would say it's phony.

It's an inconvenient truth that there is magical thinking in the New Testament. Even if Jesus didn't speak the words we find in the fake ending of Mark, the verses I quoted at the start of the chapter reflect the superstitions of the day. Even devout Christians have moved beyond these ideas. I don't know many believers who claim to cast out demons, nor would they attempt laying on of hands to cure sick friends. They take them to a doctor instead. There are fringe groups that *speak in tongues*, but not much of that goes on in most churches. Nor are drinking poison and picking up snakes considered marks of superior faith.

So, it's not a problem for mainstream Christians to ignore this strange text in Mark 16, no matter if all these feats are supposedly possible through the magic of Jesus' name. But communion and prayer are not on the periphery of faith. And the words of Jesus—the blood and flesh magic potions in John and the unrealistic promises about prayer—are additional examples of teachings that believers find it necessary to ignore or explain away.

Devout Christians aren't about to give up communion and prayer, but I've never heard a Catholic say the communion wine tasted like blood. And even the most devout and full-of-faith believers secretly know there are some things—no matter how good and important they are—they should never pray for because such prayers would yield no results.

And it's my suspicion that most Christians, if given a choice, would rather Jesus had omitted his extreme teachings about these two key disciplines of faith.

8 - I Don't Want Everyone to Understand Me

Jesus doesn't want everyone to understand him, nor does he want everyone to repent. But he does want believers to take his message to all people and to challenge them to become his disciples (followers who learn from the teacher). If you are confused and perplexed by the words of Jesus below, you are not alone.

> **When he was alone, those who were around him along with the twelve asked him about the parables. And he said to them, 'To you has been given the secret [or mystery] of the kingdom of God, but for those outside, everything comes in parables; in order that 'they may indeed look, but not perceive, and may indeed listen, but not understand; so that they may not turn again and be forgiven.' (Mark 4:10-12, NRSV)**

These last couple of lines in quotation marks are based on Isaiah 6:10 (NRSV):

> Make the mind of this people dull,
> and stop their ears,

and shut their eyes,
so that they may not look with their eyes,
and listen with their ears,
and comprehend with their minds,
and turn and be healed.

In this chapter, the prophet describes his psychedelic vision of God sitting on a throne. God wants Isaiah to promise widespread destruction to Israel—his wrath will not abate "until cities lie waste without inhabitant, and houses without men, and the land is utterly desolate"[19] Mark's use of this frightful text offers insight into his apocalyptic mindset about how scary the approaching Kingdom will be. And it's a reminder that the ferocious God of the Old Testament has not left the scene.

For a long time, devout New Testament scholars have been stressed about Mark 4:10-12. How could their beloved Jesus *not* want *all* people to repent? So, there has been a lot of discussion about this "Messianic Secret." Jesus promises he will explain the secret meaning of his parables to the disciples. They can breathe a sigh of relief. But that doesn't solve the problem we see here, and neither has all the theological explaining generated by these words. This remains a text to stumble over. And verse 34 doesn't help:

> **...he did not speak to them except in parables, but he explained everything in private to his disciples. (Mark 4:34, NRSV)**

---

[19] Isaiah 6:11 NRSV.

We usually think of parables as stories told to make a point, not to hide something. In other passages, Jesus uses parables to convey great moral lessons, and these are not hard to figure out, for example, the parable of the Good Samaritan.

Moreover, Mark 4:34 doesn't align well with Jesus' preaching as described in John's gospel, where he doesn't teach in parables at all. Instead, we find long Jesus monologues—characterized by clear and direct statements—that are missing in the other gospels.

And this is not the only striking contrast between John's gospel and the other three gospels. While some individuals are under the curse of having the world's most important truths hidden from them so they will not understand and repent, those on the good side of Jesus have a special promise: The Holy Spirit will teach them everything they need to know:

> **But the Advocate, the Holy Spirit, whom the Father will send in my name, will teach you everything, and remind you of all that I have said to you. (John 14:26, NRSV)**

Which is it? Is it the role of the Holy Spirit to teach "everything"? Or is the Holy Spirit busy sowing confusion to pursue the goal of keeping people in the dark?

In Christian history, there has been so much disagreement about the Holy Spirit's message. Right at the start, Christians couldn't agree on the essentials of basic doctrines. There seems to have been a lot of variations on the message, as Paul complained:

> **For if someone comes and proclaims another Jesus than the one we proclaimed, or if you receive a different spirit from the one you received, or a different gospel from the one you accepted, you submit to it readily enough. (II Corinthians 11:4, NRSV)**

Paul wrote that he opposed Peter "to his face, because he stood self-condemned."[20] Why? Because Peter, the number one disciple who spent one to three years in 24/7 on the job training with Jesus, did not agree with Paul's way of seeing the faith. There are now more than 30,000 different Christian brands because Christians can't agree on what God is like, what he wants humans to do, and how he wants to be worshipped. Was Jesus wrong in expecting that the Holy Spirit would keep everyone correctly informed?

And it's not just that God doesn't want some people to understand the truth. Apparently, he also doesn't not want even his most loyal followers thinking too much. Jesus idealizes childhood, that stage in human development when critical thinking is least likely to occur. He seems to be saying that *understanding* is of far less value than *credulity*.

> **Truly I tell you, unless you change and become like children, you will never enter the kingdom**

[20] Galatians 2:11, NRSV.

> **of heaven. Whoever becomes humble like this child is the greatest in the kingdom of heaven. (Matthew 18:3-4, NRSV)**

The gospels were written well before critical thinking—especially about religion—had come into fashion, well before due diligence and fact-checking were common practice, and before literacy among the common people was widespread. But even today, religions—not just Christianity—are good at aiming their appeals at people who will simply believe and comply. What better audience, in fact, than children, who generally trust parents and authority figures, and adults who have similar levels of naiveté?

Adopting a childlike compliance is not optional. Jesus issued a threat: *You will never enter the kingdom of heaven if you don't do this.*

If you value the knowledge that is acquired only by careful study and critical thinking, you must be troubled by these teachings of Jesus. Surely this can't be right: Some people don't get to understand, and those who do get to understand must remember they are called to be spoon-fed when it comes to what they know.

If God, who is proclaimed as all-knowing and all-powerful, wanted everyone to understand who he is and what he expects of them, wouldn't everyone understand who he is and what he expects of them?

9 - Do What I Say or I Will Hurt You

I am pretty sure the first Bible verse I learned by heart was John 3:16, probably because my mother was so fond of it. As you read the verse, think about how it impacts the mind of a child who is introduced to it as "the truth from God himself."

> **For God so loved the world that he gave his only Son, so that everyone who believes in him may not perish but may have eternal life. (John 3:16, NRSV)**

John 3:16 remains a Christian favorite, perhaps largely because of the way it's drilled into the consciousness of children in Sunday School. For many believers, it captures the essence of the New Testament, and occasionally we see fans at sporting events holding up signs, "John 3:16." Upon reflection, however, this verse has some weaknesses, and the reasoning behind it should give us reason to question its theology.

"Gave his son" seems like a good thing: God sent his son to bring the good news to humans. But "gave his son" is a reference to the human sacrifice required by God to enable him to forgive sins. This idea seems to be a relic of ancient superstitions, as scholar Hector Avalos has points out:

> Christ's sacrifice is premised on the sort of blood-magic inherited from the ancient Near East. Christian apologists might claim their god has the authority to order sacrifice, but their claim is no more verifiable than that of any other religion that practices human sacrifice.[21]

I do wonder why Christians aren't put off by this barbaric feature at the heart of their theology. Does it bother you?

Another problem with John 3:16 is that it encourages religious arrogance, the assumption that "our religion is the one true religion." That is, those who *don't believe in Jesus* are excluded from the promise of eternal life. This means that the vast majority of humans have missed out on God's love for the world. Tim Sledge has done the math:

> A few moments of simple analysis reveal that if we take the words of Jesus seriously, a clear majority of humanity is destined for an eternal address in hell. About 2.1 billion of the world's 7.5 billion people alive today identify themselves as Christians—about one out of four—which leaves more than 5 billion people headed for hell. When you apply even a remotely similar ratio to previous

---

[21] Hector Avalos, in his essay "Yahweh Is a Moral Monster," in *The Christian Delusion: Why Faith Fails*, edited by John w. Loftus, p. 227.

> millennia, according to the Gospels, an all-powerful, all-loving God created a world in which most of the beings made in his image are destined for torture—torture so extreme it would cause instant death in this mortal life.[22]

So there is a severity here that many of the faithful seem not to notice—but it's right there two verses later in John 3:18 (NRSV):

> **Those who believe in him are not condemned; but those who do not believe are condemned already, because they have not believed in the name of the only Son of God.**

This sinister thought is driven home by the last verse of John 3:

> **Whoever believes in the Son has eternal life; whoever disobeys the Son will not see life, but must endure God's wrath. (John 3:36, NRSV)**

These verses undermine the assumption that God's love is the essence of the New Testament. The wrath of God, so prominent in the Old Testament, is right here as well. And anyone who reads the letters of Paul can easily pick up on his certainty that *wrath* is God's default emotion.

---

[22] Tim Sledge, *Goodbye Jesus: An Evangelical Preacher's Journey Beyond Faith* (Houston: Insighting Growth Publications, 2018, Second Edition), p. 340.

As an aside, by the way, are John 3:16 and 3:36 the words of Jesus? In my old Revised Standard Version—the very one I used as a teenager—John 3:16 is printed in red, so most readers would assume Yes. But John 3:36 is not printed in red and has this footnote: "Some interpreters hold that the quotation continues through verse 36." What's this about?

New Testament Greek manuscripts do not have punctuation marks, e.g., periods, commas, quotation marks, etc. So, translators and editors add punctuation as required by modern English—and they sometimes disagree. We can't know for sure if John meant all of John 3 to be a Jesus quote.

But no matter if 3:16 and 3:36 are the words of Jesus or simply the words of John, the author, the *wrath motif* is by no means rare in the teachings of Jesus. So, it's no exaggeration to assert that his attitude was: D*o what I say, or I will hurt you.*

At the end of Chapter One, I mentioned Jesus' promise to his disciples that the villages and towns that refused to listen to their preaching would be burned to the ground on the day of judgment. You can't be more explicit than that: *I will hurt you*. But the same brutal message is found in Matthew 25, the Last Judgment scene. Folks tend to focus here on one of the most cherished texts in the Bible:

> **...the righteous will answer him, 'Lord, when was it that we saw you hungry and gave you food, or thirsty and gave you something to drink? And when was it that we saw you a**

> **stranger and welcomed you, or naked and gave you clothing? And when was it that we saw you sick or in prison and visited you?' And the king will answer them, 'Truly I tell you, just as you did it to one of the least of these my brothers, you did it to me.' (Matthew 25:37-40, NRSV)**

Those who have done these good deeds are privileged to "inherit the kingdom," but others are not so lucky:

> **Then he will say to those at his left hand, 'You that are accursed, depart from me into the *eternal fire* prepared for the devil and his angels; for I was hungry and you gave me no food, I was thirsty and you gave me nothing to drink, I was a stranger and you did not welcome me, naked and you did not give me clothing, sick and in prison and you did not visit me.' Then they also will answer, 'Lord, when was it that we saw you hungry or thirsty or a stranger or naked or sick or in prison, and did not take care of you?' Then he will answer them, 'Truly I tell you, just as you did not do it to one of the least of these, you did not do it to me.' And these will go away into *eternal punishment*, but the righteous into eternal life." (Matthew 25:41-46, NRSV)**

This can't be right: the people who *fall short on a high and consistent level of compassion* get tossed into eternal fire? Even many devout Christians would confess that they don't measure up by this standard. And isn't it too bad that quite a few categories of sinners aren't included in this list of those who deserve eternal fire? What about slave owners, child abusers, murderers, and rapists?

It's easy for religious doctrine to stumble over itself and get into a hopeless tangle. In John 3:16, we read that those who believe in the son of God win eternal life, but in Matthew 25, "inheriting the kingdom" is based on feeding the hungry, clothing the naked, and visiting those in prison.

My guess is that many Christians feel in their gut that you get to heaven if you've been a kind, decent person. So, what happens to people who feed the hungry, clothe the naked, and visit prisoners but *don't believe* in Jesus? Do they get a free pass?

There are more *I will hurt you* warnings in Jesus' teachings. Christians have dutifully prayed—following Jesus' instructions—for his kingdom to come. And they assume that it will be wonderful, but Jesus had something else in mind:

> **For as the days of Noah were, so will be the coming of the Son of Man. For as in those days before the flood they were eating and drinking, marrying and giving in marriage, until the day Noah entered the ark, and they knew nothing until the flood came and swept them all away, so too will be the coming of the Son of Man. (Matthew 24:37-39, NRSV)**

That's pretty bad: except for one family and the animals on the ark, everything in the world was drowned in "the days of Noah." There's more of the same in Mark 13:

> **For in those days there will be suffering, such as has not been from the beginning of the creation that God created until now, no, and never will be. And if the Lord had not cut short those days, no one would be saved; but for the sake of the elect, whom he chose, he has cut short those days. (Mark 13:19-20, NRSV)**

These texts make the coming kingdom—the arrival of the son of man, Jesus himself coming on the clouds[23]—sound pretty grim, with plenty of hurt. Many Christians lean on a belief that they will all be snatched away from the earth before all this misery starts, but if that's true, why the words: "...but for the sake of the elect, whom he chose, he has cut short those days."[24]

It's tough to hang on to "God so loved the world" when we read passages like these, especially the whole of Mark 13, which has been called the Little Apocalypse because of the upheaval it describes. It has to be one of the most troubling chapters in the New Testament. How does it fit in a favorable picture of Jesus?

---

[23] Mark 14 62.

[24] Some theologians have based their belief in predestination on this text, seeing "the elect" as referring to those designated for heaven right from birth, but it could also mean that, for Jesus, "the elect" are those who obey him as taught in John 3:36.

Jesus' teaching in Matthew 10 presents the same challenge:

> **Do not think that I have come to bring peace to the earth; I have not come to bring peace, but a sword. For I have come to set a man against his father, and a daughter against her mother, and a daughter-in-law against her mother-in-law; and one's foes will be members of one's own household. (Matthew 10:34-36, NRSV)**

This is a bit jarring since we're so used to the lyrics in Handel's *Messiah*, in which Isaiah 9:6 is applied to Jesus—calling him the **Prince of Peace**. Here in Matthew 10:34, Jesus spurns that identification, and the family discord depicted—too much hurt all around—seems in line with Luke's dreadful hate-your-family verse[25] that we considered in *Chapter One*.

Surely most Christians wish Jesus hadn't taught he planned to cause so much hurt.

---

[25] Luke 14:26.

10 - I Will Return During Your Lifetime

In the oldest document in the New Testament, I Thessalonians, the apostle Paul assured believers that their dead relatives—those who had converted to Christ, that is—would rise to meet Jesus in the air. Here's Paul's confident promise:

> **But we do not want you to be uninformed, brothers, about those who have died, so that you may not grieve as others do who have no hope. For since we believe that Jesus died and rose again, even so, through Jesus, God will bring with him those who have died.**
>
> **For the Lord himself, with a cry of command, with the archangel's call and with the sound of God's trumpet, will descend from heaven, and the dead in Christ will rise first. Then we who are alive, who are left, will be caught up in the clouds together with them to meet the Lord in the air; and so we will be with the Lord forever. (I Thessalonians 4:13-17, NRSV)**

This is a window into the earliest Christian thinking—at

least Paul's version of it. How can these verses not be an embarrassment? Paul was confident that he would be alive for this momentous event: "...we who are alive, who are left, will be caught up in the clouds together with them..." The imminent arrival of Jesus was a constant theme in Paul's letters.

Paul was wrong.

My question to Christians: Do you simply dismiss this mistaken prediction—no matter that it's in the New Testament? Do you really suppose Paul just got the timing wrong? Do you file this belief in that mental drawer marked, "Not Worth Thinking About (And if I did think about it, I would be disturbed, unsettled, and anxious)"? Apparently, this is what many believers do. But other Christians discount Paul's failed prediction and cherish the hope that they will see Jesus coming on the clouds. A 2010 survey showed that 41 percent of Americans expect Jesus will show up before 2050.[26]

Apocalypticism—what is being uncovered, revealed—is theology that dreams of the day when God will intervene in history to set things right, to get even. One of its forms is messianism. That is, there will be a hero to put things right, a Messiah, the Messiah, who will reverse the oppression of the Chosen People, long under the heel of foreign empires.

Thanks to Paul, apocalypticism had been planted in the

---

[26] *YNet News*, "Many Americans Expect Jesus' Return by 2050," June 23, 2010, https://www.ynetnews.com/articles/0,7340,L-3909431,00.html.

New Testament, well before the gospels had been written. Two or three decades after Paul, the gospel-movement—the effort to tell the story of Jesus in narrative form—was underway. And starting with Mark, Jesus was portrayed predicting his return, someday soon after his death, on the clouds. In other words, Mark dramatized Paul's theology.[27]

It's important to understand that the apocalypticism in the New Testament was not an isolated belief. Richard Carrier has pointed out:

> Palestine in the early first century C.E. was experiencing a rash of messianism. There was an evident clamoring of sects and individuals to announce that they had found the messiah. It is therefore no oddity or accident that this is exactly when Christianity arose. It was yet another messiah cult in the midst of a fad for just such cults.[28]

David Fitzgerald has listed about a dozen other messiah candidates. These are the ones we know about.[29] So, messianism was manifested in many guises, and in the New Testament, we find that Jesus plays the leading role. There are still Christians—41 percent of American Christians by that one poll—who have not put "Jesus

---

[27] For more on this, see Tom Dykstra, *Mark, Canonizer of Paul*.
[28] Richard Carrier, *On the Historicity of Jesus* (Sheffield: Sheffield Phoenix Press, 2014), p. 67
[29] David Fitzgerald, *Jesus: Mything in Action*, Volume 1 (Self-Published, 2016), pp. 113-120.

coming on the clouds" in that file of things not worth thinking about. We're all used to the end-of-the world preachers who keep resetting the clock for the arrival of Jesus. But these preachers ignore the timing as specified in the texts: Jesus was supposed to come back in the first century!

Apocalypticism is a relic of ancient superstition. Jesus, at his trial, tells the high priest: "You will see the Son of Man seated at the right hand of the Power and coming with the clouds of heaven." (Mark 14:62, NRSV) **Obviously, this text has been falsified by history. It didn't happen.**

But a lot of New Testament thinking got stuck here. The "clouds of heaven" is reminiscent of Paul's promise in I Thessalonians 4, cited at the beginning of this chapter, and these images show up again in the Book of Acts, where we read that the disciples witnessed Jesus ascend to heaven:

> **While he was going and they were gazing up toward heaven, suddenly two men in white robes stood by them. They said, 'Men of Galilee, why do you stand looking up toward heaven? This Jesus, who has been taken up from you into heaven, will come in the same way as you saw him go into heaven.' (Acts, 1:10-11, NRSV)**

Jesus' prediction at this trial is echoed in the words of Stephen in the moments before he was martyred:

> But filled with the Holy Spirit, he gazed into heaven and saw the glory of God and Jesus

> standing at the right hand of God. 'Look,' he said, 'I see the heavens opened and the Son of Man standing at the right hand of God!' (Acts 7:55-56, NRSV)

These have been cherished, comforting texts for Christians for a long time. **But they do not stand up to careful analysis.**

Naïve concepts of heaven (i.e., "it's up there") have been eliminated by our knowledge of our biosphere and our earth in solar orbit through space pulsing with radiation. One comic has observed:

> In the course of his ascension at around 15,000 feet Jesus began to wish he had brought a sweater. At 30,000 feet he felt weak from lack of oxygen. By 100,000 feet his bodily fluids were boiling away from every orifice. If he ever did return, it would be as a fifty-pound lump of bone and frozen jerky.[30]

Hence theologians have retreated to a metaphoric interpretation of these texts: It must mean something spiritual. When I was a teen fascinated by astronomy, I asked my mother where heaven was, and she gave an answer that worked for a while: It is a state of being, a relationship with God. So, even though very pious, she also was savvy enough to know that heaven was not out there/up there to be surveyed by telescopes and rockets. So

---

[30] Scott McKellar on Facebook.

Stephen's vision of Jesus standing next to God needs to be taken symbolically.

But it's harder to get away with a metaphorical interpretation of Jesus' prediction that those attending his trial would see the Son of Man "coming with the clouds of heaven." There was a passionate belief that the Messiah would show up, in person, real-time in the real world, to—among other things—toss out the Romans. Surely this must qualify as a major thing Christians wish Jesus hadn't taught—*even those* who still hope that Jesus is coming back. They have to keep coming up with excuses as to why all of the predictions about the timing of *the big day*—made through the centuries—have been wrong.

This waiting and wondering game began early. In Mark, Jesus promises he'll be coming on the clouds; when Matthew copied this text, he kept these words. But when Luke made his version, he deleted *arrival on the clouds*:

> **They said, "If you are the Messiah, tell us." He replied, "If I tell you, you will not believe, and if I question you, you will not answer. But from now on the Son of Man will be seated at the right hand of the power of God." All of them asked, "Are you, then, the Son of God?" He said to them, "You say that I am." Then they said, "What further testimony do we need? We have heard it ourselves from his own lips!" (Luke 22:67-71, NRSV)**

Luke's gospel was written some fifty years after

Christianity got underway. With each passing decade, it became harder to sustain the belief that Jesus would "arrive any day now." It's difficult for us to imagine how everyday people in antiquity sensed the passing of time. We monitor time with clocks and watches; we have calendars and are aware of "what year it is." We know what the 60s were like—or the 80s and 90s, and if not, we Google it. Did the common people in the late first century grasp that decades had passed since Jesus had died? When the uneducated heard the story of Jesus decades later, maybe they were still impressed by Jesus' prediction in Mark 14:62 that those at his trial would see him arriving on the clouds. Or maybe not. Perhaps that's why Luke deleted that part of the script.

It was probably inevitable that the Kingdom of God concept would be given a more spiritual nuance to escape the failure of its literal arrival. Hence, we also find this in Luke 17:

> **Once Jesus was asked by the Pharisees when the kingdom of God was coming, and he answered, "The kingdom of God is not coming with things that can be observed. Nor will they say, "Look, here it is!" or "There it is!" For, in fact, the kingdom of God is among you." (Luke 17:20-21, NRSV)**

Well, that's a change, isn't it? Not quite what Mark had in mind, but also purported to be the words of Jesus:

> **But in those days, after that suffering, the sun**

> **will be darkened, and the moon will not give its light, and stars will be falling from heaven, and the powers in the heavens will be shaken. Then they will see the Son of Man coming in clouds with great power and glory. Then he will send out the angels, and gather his elect from the four winds, from the ends of the earth to the ends of heaven. (Mark 13:24-27, NRSV)**

Theologians are masters of revision, to put it mildly. Let's face it: they make things up as they go along. Yes, the time did come when Christian thinkers sensed that Paul hadn't called it correctly: Jesus coming on the clouds—maybe that wasn't going to happen after all. At the very least, it seemed long overdue. Luke 17:21 is an adjustment to rescue the kingdom: "the kingdom of God is among you." Or the Greek can be translated, "within you." This is a feel-good saying, but what in the world did Luke mean by it? If you've heard sermons on this text, you may think you know. But where did your preacher get his/her ideas?

As world history has played out in the centuries since Luke wrote this revision, there is no evidence that any kingdom of God has been set up on earth—by Jesus or anyone else. And the range of behaviors—from very good to very bad—by self-professed Christians can make us wonder if a kingdom of God "within" is really a thing. It seems so hit or miss. Former pastor Tim Sledge has drawn attention to this, based on his experience with church folks:

> …as I thought about the range of personalities and lifestyles in any congregation I served or visited, I

> saw a bell curve of outstanding, average, and not-so-great people not dramatically different from the pattern of any human organization. Christian faith helps some individuals become better human beings—sometimes great human beings. But across the board, the results of believing in Jesus are disappointingly inconsistent.[31]

I suspect Luke didn't think through saying that the kingdom of God is "within." After all, he had an almost impossible task. He copied most of Mark's gospel, and Jesus the Apocalyptic Prophet is prominent there. At the very beginning of his ministry, in Mark 1:15, Jesus declares, "The time is fulfilled, and the kingdom of God has come near [or is at hand] repent, and believe in the good news." (NRSV) The stress here is on belief in what a preacher says—in this case, concerning the promised Kingdom of God. Apocalyptic prophets throughout history have preached the same thing: Their version of a new world order is near and about to happen. Just believe it! Jesus urged repentance because there was about to be fundamental change. The long-promised messianic upheaval was near. Mark 1:15, cited above, is the message of Mark's gospel.

Readers who flip randomly through the four gospels may fail to note that there is little ethical teaching in Mark. In fact, there's little teaching at all. Tom Dykstra has quoted scholar Jesper Svartvik: "Mark is remarkably uninterested

---

[31] Tim Sledge, *Four Disturbing Questions with One Simple Answer: Breaking the Spell of Christian Belief* (Houston: Insighting Growth Publications, 2019), p. 17.

in relating the teachings of Jesus. He often states that Jesus taught, but the reader seldom learns what the teaching is." To which Dykstra adds, "One of the most striking features of the second gospel is that it promises to present a 'gospel' that consists of what Jesus taught, but it never delivers on that promise."[32]

The lack of specifics is bad enough, but it gets worse. We find this later in the first chapter of Mark:

> **In the morning, while it was still very dark, he got up and went out to a deserted place, and there he prayed. And Simon and his companions hunted for him. When they found him, they said to him, 'Everyone is searching for you.' He answered, 'Let us go on to the neighboring towns, so that I may proclaim the message there also; for that is what I came out to do.' And he went throughout Galilee, proclaiming the message in their synagogues and casting out demons. (Mark 1:35-39, NRSV)**

The gospel of Mark could be subtitled "Jesus and the Demons" because its author was far more interested in positioning Jesus as a hero from the spiritual realm—who would thus play a major role in the upcoming apocalypse—rather than as a moral instructor. Mark presents Jesus the Exorcist, who could arm-wrestle with

---

[32] Tom Dykstra, *Mark, Canonizer of Paul*, (St. Paul: OCABS Press, 2012), p. 13.

demons and always win. Christians who have even a modest grasp of how the world works should be wary of this portrait of Jesus. If you accept Jesus as depicted in this gospel, you are well on your way to full-throttle crazy religion.

In Mark 1, Jesus says that he "came out to proclaim the message" of the kingdom, and its immediacy is unmistakable later in Mark: "Truly I tell you, I will never again drink of the fruit of the vine until that day when I drink it new in the kingdom of God."[33] This statement is thoroughly apocalyptic. Jesus utters these words at the Last Supper, indicating how near at hand the Kingdom of God is.

These writers who dabbled in apocalyptic delusion were confused about the timing of the end. In Matthew, when Jesus sends his disciples out to preach, he tells them: "...for truly I tell you, you will not have gone through all the towns of Israel before the Son of Man comes."[34]

Luke includes this Jesus quote: "**But truly I tell you, there are some standing here who will not taste death before they see the kingdom of God.**"[35] Surely many Christians regret Jesus taught this. Again, this is simply wrong. It didn't happen. There's more of the same: **"You also must be ready, for the Son of Man is coming at an**

---

[33] Mark 14:25, NRSV.
[34] Matthew 10:23, NRSV.
[35] Luke 9:27, NRSV.

unexpected hour."[36]

For readers in the late first century, this would have been taken as a warning to remain alert and prepared—any day now! That Jesus would take his own sweet time to show up—say, another two thousand years—would have been unthinkable. How could that have been a source of comfort or encouragement? Especially since the expulsion of the Romans would have been a keenly desired result of Jesus' arrival.

And then there are a few peculiar items

> **Truly I tell you, at the renewal of all things, when the Son of Man is seated on the throne of his glory, you who have followed me will also sit on twelve thrones, judging the twelve tribes of Israel. (Matthew 19:28, NRSV)**

This sounds like a line from a fantasy novel—or science fiction. The gospel writers apparently didn't check their own storylines for consistency. Surely this is a blunder: You who have followed me will also sit on twelve thrones? Twelve? This would suggest that Jesus hadn't yet figured out that Judas wasn't really on the team.

And here are two Jesus sayings in the same chapter of Mark that can't both be true. "**And the good news must first be proclaimed to all nations..."**[37] This is something which would not happen for a long time. And "...**Truly I**

---

[36] Luke 12:40, NRSV.
[37] Mark 13:10, NRSV.

tell you, this generation will not pass away until all these things have taken place."[38]

In the centuries following Jesus, we have seen missionary zeal to proclaim the Christian message to "all nations" translated into colonialism and the subjugation of native peoples. Indeed, Mark 13:10 has led to a disaster, inciting zealots to reach all nations in order to hasten the day when the Kingdom of God will be initiated. But verse 10 is hardly consistent with the promise of verse 30, that it will all happen before this generation passes away.

Here's another warning, addressed to the original audience of the gospel—a warning that would not make sense with an anticipated 2,000-year wait. Such a delay would have been unimaginable, inexplicable.

> **Beware, keep alert. For you do not know when the time will come. It is like a man going on a journey, when he leaves home and puts his slaves in charge, each with his work, and commands the doorkeeper to be on the watch. Therefore, keep awake—for you do not know when the master of the house will come, in the evening, or at midnight, or at cockcrow, or at dawn, or else he may find you asleep when he comes suddenly. And what I say to you I say to all: Keep awake. (Mark 13:33-37, NRSV)**

Such texts could be labeled as theological terrorism. This

---

[38] Mark 13:30, NRSV.

is an especially loathsome aspect of Christian theology, and indeed apologists have struggled with it for a long time.

I suspect this grim theology is foreign to many Christians who are fairly well adjusted to a modern worldview—and are far more concerned to save for retirement than remaining alert for the any-day-now return of Jesus. They probably don't give much thought to it—even when they come across these texts—because they don't want to admit that Jesus was simply wrong.

Apocalyptic theology is firmly embedded in the "good news" that Jesus preached. Yes, the hate-your-family verse in Luke is pretty bad, but Jesus being totally wrong about how human history would unfold is arguably worse. And we don't see any movement afoot to edit the New Testament to get rid of it. If you are a follower of Jesus, you owe it to yourself to see how far downhill New Testament theology went, with the help of words attributed to Jesus himself.[39]

****

This wraps up our look at ten teachings of Jesus that many—if not most—Christians wish Jesus hadn't taught. And many believers display little awareness that Jesus said these things. One reason for this is that many of the faithful

---

[39] A classic study of this is Bart Ehrman's *Jesus: Apocalyptic Prophet of the New Millennium*. I also recommend John W. Loftus' essay, "At Best Jesus Was a Failed Apocalyptic Prophet" in his anthology, *The Christian Delusion: Why Faith Fails*.

neglect to read the gospels carefully. One survey revealed that only about a third of Americans have read the whole Bible.[40] This is hardly a surprise when there is so much available to entertain us—sports, films, TV, etc. Then too, great stretches of the Bible aren't easy reading. So, I can't fault folks for trusting their priests and pastors to let them know what's important in the scriptures. But chances are, the clergy know these embarrassing Jesus quotes all too well and see little need to mention them from the pulpit, or perhaps just aren't comfortable talking about them.

The clergy know another troubling fact. At least many of them found this out during their seminary training: Even devout Bible scholars have known for a long time—and admit it—that Matthew, Mark, Luke, and John aren't biographies of Jesus. They don't qualify as history. So, we need to look at that problem as well.

[40] Lifeway Research: "Americans Are Fond of the Bible, Don't Actually Read It," April 25, 2017, https://lifewayresearch.com/2017/04/25/lifeway-research-americans-are-fond-of-the-bible-dont-actually-read-it/.

Part 2 - Other Reasons to Question

11 - Four Obstacles to Knowing What Jesus Said

In 2004, devout Christian scholar Ben Witherington III published a 400-page commentary on the apostle Paul's Letter to the Romans.[41] It includes a 19-page bibliography of other works about Paul and his writings, and Witherington said, "…this list could go on for miles." Indeed, the output of scholars—the results of their intensive study of the New Testament for decades—is nothing short of phenomenal.

It's not a stretch to say that the gospels have been examined more thoroughly than any other documents in Western history. The motivation, of course, has been to understand God's word—and literally, there's not a sentence in the New Testament that hadn't been carefully analyzed down to the very last syllable, many times over.

But there's been a major downside to these studies. It turns out that the gospels are not reliable biographies of Jesus,

---

[41] Ben Witherington III with Darlene Hyatt, *Paul's Letter to the Romans: A Socio-Rhetorical Commentary* (Grand Rapids: Wm. B. Eerdmans Publishing Co., 2004).

as had been assumed for centuries. In fact, the gospels display several major weaknesses, and even devout scholars have wrestled with—and agonized over—the problems that the gospels present. Even if you are a very devout Christian, I suspect that you are largely unaware of this enormous scholarly output. Ministers and priests have had some exposure to it at seminary, but even they don't keep up, and they don't always talk about all they know. *So, this downside is below the horizon of awareness of almost everyone.*

With so much about the gospels that's been written, spoken, and debated, where do we even start? Let's keep it simple and look at four easily understandable obstacles that make it hard to get at the real Jesus.

Missing: The Sources Required for Writing History

To have any shot at writing accurate accounts, historians search for documents that are *contemporaneous with events they report*. For example, a historian writing to correctly depict Lincoln's day at Gettysburg on November 19, 1863, would examine sources like letters, diaries, newspaper accounts, and White House archive materials—all written *within days* of Lincoln's famous address. This is the routine protocol followed by professional historians—the only acceptable practice.

So, historians specify, in detail, where they found their information. For example, A. Scott Berg's 743-page biography, *Wilson*, includes 38 pages of sources and notes. Helen Langdon's 391-page *Caravaggio: A Life* includes

27 pages of sources and notes.

No such references exist for the Jesus story. The four gospels were written decades after the events depicted, and not once do their authors provide specific details about their sources. It's easy to be misled by the opening verses of Luke's account:

> Since many have undertaken to set down an orderly account of the events that have been fulfilled among us, just as they were handed on to us by those who from the beginning were eyewitnesses and servants of the word, I too decided, after investigating everything carefully from the very first, to write an orderly account for you, most excellent Theophilus, so that you may know the truth concerning the things about which you have been instructed. (Luke 1:1-4, NRSV)

"...handed on to us by those who from the beginning were eyewitnesses", "...after investigating everything carefully from the very first." Sounds legit, right?

Yet, the precise sources are not cited. The very thing historians need is missing. If Luke wrote sixty to seventy years after the death of Jesus, it's smart positioning, of course, to claim his account is based on eyewitness reports. But making the claim doesn't make it a fact—nor does it mean we should believe it.

If you don't identify your sources and cite contemporaneous documentation, the story doesn't

qualify as history.

And this is crucial: Luke borrowed wide swaths of text from Mark's gospel—without mentioning that he did so. Today we call this plagiarism, even if Luke labeled it "events handed on to us." But the author of Mark himself was at least forty years removed from the scene and didn't identify *his* sources either. We're not impressed if Mark was one of Luke's "eyewitnesses." Even Luke didn't altogether trust Mark's text and freely reworked it when he saw fit.

Moreover, after Luke's eloquent claim that he "investigated everything," what does he give us? He begins his gospel with an account of a decades-old event featuring angels and heavenly hosts in speaking roles and continues with a genealogy tracing Jesus' ancestry back to Adam! (Luke 3:23-38). What's missing here? An explanation of how Luke knew these events happened! So, of course, the response of professional historians is: "No! This won't do!"

The claim that the gospels "tell it like it was" has also been based on the last two verses of John's gospel, a reference to this gospel's author, the so-called beloved disciple:

> This is the disciple who is testifying to these things and has written them, and we know that his testimony is true. But there are also many other things that Jesus did; if every one of them were written down, I suppose that the world itself could not contain the books that would be written. (John

21:24-25, NRSV)

Any fiction writer could tag on a claim like this, especially when writing several decades later. And nothing is said about the precise sources and *contemporaneous documentation* that the "disciple who is testifying" may have used.

It is the consensus of New Testament scholars—as much as anything can be—that John was the last gospel to be written. And to those of us outside the Christian camp, it's clear that John had a tendency to exaggerate. Or, to put it more bluntly, John seems to have been a prodigious inventor of new doctrines about Jesus. Ironically, John's gospel undermines its own credibility because—compared to the other three—*it says too much.*

For example, why do the other gospel writers fail to include the lengthy Jesus monologues we find in John? Were they not paying attention, or did John's author just make them up? Embellishing the story was common practice in the ancient world when authors wrote stories about heroes. Less politely, it seems that John was dishonest, as Richard Carrier has stated bluntly:

> John's Gospel contains long, implausible, never-before-imagined speeches of Jesus (and yet, no Sermon on the Mount, or indeed hardly any moral instruction of any sort), and entirely new characters and events also never heard of before (Nicodemus, Lazarus, Cana)… John has run wild with authorial gluttony, freely changing

> everything and inventing whatever he wants. By modern standards, John is lying.[42]

Carrier points out that the other gospels do not mention a Beloved Disciple, and, again, he identifies this as a ploy:

> John has clearly 'inserted' this figure into these stories he inherited from the Synoptics, and then claimed this new character as his 'source' who saw all these things (21:24). In plain terms, that's simply a lie.[43]

Professional historians know that contemporaneous documentation—letters, diaries, transcriptions—would be required to verify John's "authorial gluttony" displayed throughout his gospel, composed so many years after Jesus.

Here's something else to bear in mind. We have no way of knowing when the words of Jesus were first written down or how those who heard him would have done so. Jesus is depicted as wildly popular, drawing huge crowds. But we can assume there weren't stenographers following him around. The overwhelming majority of those who heard him were illiterate, so even if they wanted to write down what Jesus said, they couldn't have done so. And who carried around the ancient equivalents of pads of paper and pencils? And without sound systems like we have today,

---

[42] Richard Carrier, *On the Historicity of Jesus: Why We Might Have Reason for Doubt*, pp. 490-491.
[43] Richard Carrier, *On the Historicity of Jesus: Why We Might Have Reason for Doubt*, p. 500.

it's hard to imagine how many in his audiences could clearly hear and understand what he was saying.

It may be argued that some of Jesus' sayings were jotted down later. I sure wouldn't like to be given this challenge: to write down, without any errors, even a few sentences of the sermon after coming home from church. Hours or days later, could people have recalled Jesus' words with dead accuracy? Then how would these scraps of reminiscences have ended up in the hands of the gospel authors decades later? We should be properly skeptical that we have the *actual words of Jesus* in the gospels.

It will be argued by some Christians that the words of Jesus in the gospels are true because God inspired the authors. That alone guarantees authenticity. But we can see very plainly when we compare the gospels, that Matthew and Luke freely altered the Jesus script they found in Mark as they saw fit, which betrays an imperfect process. Even devout scholars struggle with the many contradictions found in the gospels. It's awkward to attribute this confusion to God.

Moreover, "God inspired the authors to tell the truth" is actually a form of *special pleading*. That is, the gospels are exempt from the rules of writing accurate history, "…because our faith is true." Other religions indulge in the same special pleading. Would Christians grant this privilege to Muslims and Mormons who make the same claim for their scriptures? Special pleading is a form of wishful thinking: "I want these words of Jesus to be real, so I'm sure God inspired the authors."

The search for truth is not based on this kind of faith bias. Frankly, those outside the faith suspect that Christians who make this argument are trying to pull a fast one. It looks too much like cheating—because it is.

Missing: The Intent to Write History

Most Christians regard the gospels as "stories of Jesus"—which is true. They are ***stories***, but they fail to measure up as history for the reasons mentioned above. It's not hard to detect, moreover, that the agenda of the gospel authors was theology, and every story was designed to serve that agenda.

For example, consider how Matthew reworked Mark's simple two-verse description of the temptation of Jesus. This is all Mark said about it: "And the Spirit immediately drove him out into the wilderness. He was in the wilderness forty days, tempted by Satan; and he was with the wild beasts; and the angels waited on him."[44]

Historians wince at these verses for three reasons:

- "Forty days in the wilderness" looks like an attempt to mimic Israel's years of wandering.
- And who was watching all this, counting the days?
- Satan is a figure borrowed from other ancient

---

[44] Mark 1:12-13, NRSV.

mythologies, and angels are in the same category.

Matthew expanded this to eleven verses and presents a conversation between Jesus and the Satan, with the latter whisking Jesus (à la Superman?) to the top of the Jerusalem Temple and to a "very high" mountaintop from which they could survey all the kingdoms of the earth. Jesus refused all the devil's offers.

This was in the wilderness, so we can be sure no one was there taking notes on the conversation! Not for a moment can historians regard this as history. Maybe Jesus told his disciples about it later? That's speculation, and without *contemporaneous documentation*, this suggestion carries no weight. It's much more likely that it came out of Matthew's theologically fired imagination. *What actually happened didn't matter.*

Matthew was also a literary creator and invented freely. The treasured Sermon on the Mount was his attempt to make up for the lack of moral teaching in Mark's gospel. Richard Carrier's insights here are crucial. He notes that the Sermon on the Mount

> …is a well-crafted literary work that cannot have come from some illiterate Galilean. In fact, we know it originated in Greek, not Hebrew or Aramaic, because it relies on the Septuagint text of the Bible for all its feature and allusions. It relies extensively on the Greek text of Deuteronomy and Leviticus especially…

> These are not the words of Jesus. This famous sermon as a whole also has a complex literary structure that can only have come from a *writer*, not an everyday speaker.[45]

Without the intent to write history, the gospel authors built their stories with the primary source—other than their imaginations—at hand, namely, the Old Testament. It was here, they were certain, that texts could be found to build their Jesus stories—and they were creative.

For example, Jesus miraculously feeding the huge crowds in Mark 6 and 8 is an expansion of Elijah's miracle in II Kings 4:42-44. The account of Jesus dying on the cross in Mark 15:34-36 pulls verses from Psalms 22 and 69.[46] Since the gospel authors were confident Jesus was the messiah—the son of God—how could ingredients of his story *not* be found in the Old Testament? That was their theological bias.

All of the gospels, bear in mind, were written after the destruction of Jerusalem in 70 C.E. and well after the lifetimes of most of those who had known Jesus. Where else to find "information" about Jesus, other than in God's ancient writings, as David Chumney has pointed out:

> Our primary source of information about Jesus'

---

[45] Richard Carrier, *On the Historicity of Jesus*, pp. 465-466.
[46] See especially, Robert M. Price, *The Christ-Myth Theory and Its Problems*, for a thorough list of Old Testament texts and their gospel parallels.

> arrest and crucifixion is what is reported in the Gospels. The passion narrative in Mark's gospel—the foundation for what is found in the other three—is comprised largely of allusions to the Old Testament...But why did Mark rely so heavily on such material? He did do, critics have concluded, because that is all he had.[47]

One of the classic treatments of this issue is Randel Helms' 1988 book, *Gospel Fictions*:

> Each of the four canonical Gospels is religious proclamation in the form of a largely fictional narrative. Christians have never been reluctant to write fiction about Jesus, and we must remember that our four canonical Gospels are only the cream of a large and varied literature.[48]
>
> The Gospels are Hellenistic religious narratives in the tradition of the Greek Septuagint version of the Old Testament, which constituted the "Scriptures" to those Greek-speaking Christians who wrote the four canonical Gospels and who appealed to it, explicitly or implicitly, in nearly every paragraph

---

[47] David Chumney, *Eclipsing Jesus: How Searching the Scriptures Got in the Way of Recounting the Facts (North Charleston: CreateSpace Independent Publishing Platform, 2017),* Kindle Loc 11696.

[48] Randel Helms, *Gospel Fictions* (Amherst: Prometheus Books, Reprint Edition, 1989), p. 11.

> they wrote.[49]

Helms also quotes Northrop Frye:

> Evidence, so called, is bounced back and forth between the testaments like a tennis ball; and no other evidence is given us. The two testaments form a double mirror, each reflecting the other but neither the world outside.[50]

The gospel authors may have intended, on some level, to tell their readers about Jesus, but theology was their primary task. They failed to deliver what we would consider history because *that wasn't the goal.* Indeed, R. G. Price argues that the author of Mark was creating allegory from the get-go, and that the other gospel writers failed to realize this:

> What the Gospel of Mark is, is a fictional allegory that was likely written sometime between 70 and 80 C.E. in reaction to the First Jewish-Roman War and the sacking of Jerusalem by the Romans. Virtually every scene in this story is built on literary allusions to the Hebrew scriptures. These literary allusions were interpreted, however, as examples of prophecy fulfillment by later readers,

---

[49] Randel Helms, *Gospel Fictions*, p. 16.
[50] Randel Helms, *Gospel Fictions*, p. 19, citing Northrop Frye, *The Great Code: The Bible and Literature*, 1982, p. 78.

> including writers of the other Gospels.
>
> That every account of Jesus' life is dependent on this one story, and that the events of Jesus' life in this story originate from literary allusions, means that no account of the life of Jesus is based on any real events or any real person.
>
> ...the entire case for Christianity is revealed to be nothing more than a huge literary misunderstanding.[51]

Perhaps the most significant misunderstanding we're dealing with here is the assumption that the gospel writers were trying to be historians.

The historical Jesus is not easy to find, but even so, most secular historians accept that Jesus existed. That yes, he was a real person. But that doesn't mean Christians can breathe a sigh of relief. Priests and preachers don't make a habit of keeping laypeople up to date on debates raging in New Testament academia—and indeed, there has been considerable debate about what can be known about Jesus. No one has developed a reliable method for identifying genuine history in the gospels. Hence there have been many different "Jesus proposals," i.e., who and what he actually was—and precious little agreement. Most of these scholars, bear in mind, are devout and have an emotional investment in getting to the bottom of this "Jesus

---

[51] R. G. Price, *Deciphering the Gospels Proves Jesus Never Existed*, (Self-Published, 2018), pp. xx-xxi.

problem." Most of the folks in the pews are unaware of these problems that plague any serious Jesus study.

While belief in the man from Galilee has two thousand years of momentum and seems such a certainty, there is so much uncertainty, on top of which there has been the suspicion—in some circles—that Jesus may have been a mythical invention. This speculation can be traced at least to the 18th century,[52] so the Jesus Mythicism movement that has gained attention in recent years is nothing new—and is far from being a fad.

I urge you to avoid knee-jerk reactions like, "Of course, Jesus existed, don't be silly." There is indignation at the very idea that Jesus might not have existed, ***but not enough curiosity***. Please do some homework. Find out why there are doubts that Jesus ever lived. Bring some understanding to the debate. I'm a little suspicious of Christians who flame out on this issue but who cannot cite any of the hard facts that point to a mythical Jesus.

Rise to the challenge of being able to discuss the topic intelligently. Even scholars who are confident that Jesus existed wrestle with these difficulties:

- Even devout scholars admit there is no contemporaneous documentation at all for anything Jesus said or did.

---

[52] *Wikipedia*, "Christ Myth Theory," Referenced August, 2021, https://en.wikipedia.org/wiki/Christ_myth_theory#Late_18th_to_early_20th_century.

- The teachings and deeds of Jesus—even his miracles reported in the gospels—are not mentioned in the New Testament epistles written well before the gospels.
- There is so much folklore, fantasy, superstition, and magical thinking in the gospels. What are the implications of this when we're trying to figure out who Jesus really was, on the assumption that he existed?
- As of yet, no reliable methodology has been developed for identifying, for sure, which gospels stories are actually historical. Exactly where are the certain tidbits of history in the gospels? Gospel experts have arrived at no consensus.

So, it's complicated, which is no surprise since we're trying to determine what happened in the first century. I urge you to dig into a few of the basic books on Jesus Mythicism published just in the last few years:

- Earl Doherty, *Jesus: Neither God Nor Man: The Case for a Mythical Jesus*
- Richard Carrier, *On the Historicity of Jesus: Why We Might Have Reason for Doubt*
- Richard Carrier, *Jesus from Outer Space: What the Earliest Christians Really Believed About Christ*
- David Fitzgerald, *Nailed: Ten Christian Myths that Show that Jesus Never Existed at All*
- David Fitzgerald, *Jesus: Mything in Action* (3 volumes)
- Raphael Lataster, *Jesus Did Not Exist: A Debate*

Among Atheists
- Raphael Lataster, *There Was No Jesus, There Is No God: A Scholarly Examination of the Scientific, Historical, and Philosophical Evidence & Arguments for Monotheism*
- R. G. Price, *Deciphering the Gospels Proves Jesus Never Existed*

Missing: Verification of Oral Tradition

With no contemporaneous documentation to work with—no paper trail backing up the gospel accounts—devout scholars have nursed the fond hope that stories about Jesus and his teaching were *faithfully and accurately remembered.* What else do they have to go on to counter the suspicion that the gospel writers just made stuff up? Isn't it a fatal wound to the faith—if Randal Helms got it right with the title of his book: *Gospel Fictions?*

But what are the chances that *reliable oral tradition* is a thing? What can happen as stories are repeated over the course of forty years, retold dozens or even hundreds of times? Oral tradition, Helms points out, "...is by definition unstable, notoriously open to mythical, legendary, and fictional embellishment."[53] Tom Dykstra has a chapter titled "The Chimera of Oral Tradition" in his book,[54] and he also identifies the problem:

> Besides the lack of evidence, the problem here is the allowance for "reflections and interpretations":

---

[53] Randel Helms, *Gospel Fictions,* p. 12.
[54] Tom Dykstra, *Mark, Canonizer of Paul*, pp. 41-65.

> add those up over 30 years and what you have at the end may have little to do with what you started with.[55]

Dykstra also notes that the apostle Paul was annoyed that his congregation in Galatia had heard a version of the gospel different than the one he has preached:

> The epistle to the Galatians bears witness to the development of "oral traditions" directly contradicting the gospel he had preached in Galatia, and the tradition in Galatia metamorphosed so drastically not over 30 years but within a very short time after he left…[56]

Paul is a source of even more embarrassment, however, for those who argue that oral traditions about Jesus were in circulation in the early Christian communities. He seems not to have heard of these traditions since he says almost nothing about the ministry and teachings of Jesus in his letters. How was it possible for him to be so far out of the loop if robust oral tradition was making the rounds?

With so much uncertainty about the actual words Jesus may have spoken, we should acknowledge that printing Jesus-script in red fails as a best practice. It's a form of *pious deception* and a clue that we must remain on the alert for translator bias. Almost always, Bible translators and editors are pious believers and are just as committed—as

---

[55] Tom Dykstra, Mark, *Canonizer of Paul*, p. 56.
[56] Tom Dykstra, *Mark, Canonizer of Paul*, p. 57.

the gospel authors were—to their own agendas. They want to enhance devotion to scripture.

But they must surely know that the *authentic* words of Jesus—which alone would justify printing this script in red—are subject to doubt for all the reasons I have described. Moreover, Jesus spoke Aramaic, but in the gospels, we find his words in Greek. How faithfully, how accurately, was the work of translation done with a gap of at least forty years between Jesus ***speaking*** and authors of the gospels ***writing***. Then, the original Greek manuscripts were lost, and each gospel had to be reconstructed by a careful comparison of copies that did survive. Centuries later, English translators got to work and came up with dozens of different versions. The red ink "words of Jesus" play upon the gullibility of readers unaware of this complex, tortured history.

Bear in mind also that translators have to make judgment calls based on the *lack of punctuation* in the Greek manuscripts of the gospels. There were no quotation marks, for example. Hence the translators who produced the *New International Version* did not print John 3:16-21 in red, while these verses are in red in my old *Revised Standard Version*. So, is the famous John 3:16 a Jesus quote, or is it an affirmation by the author of the gospel?

Some examples of the red ink are actually a joke. In Mark 13, Jesus is positioned on the Mount of Olives, delivering his terrible apocalyptic message to the disciples. Look at verse 14: "But when you see the desolating sacrilege set up where it ought not to be (let the reader understand), then those in Judea must flee to the mountains." (NRSV) In my old version of the RSV, the parenthetical "let the reader understand" is printed in red! So, did Jesus actually say to his disciples, "Let ***the reader*** understand"? No. We can assume these words were added to the text by a copyist spooked by the harsh message of Mark 13. And in I Corinthians 11, when Paul reports the words of Jesus to him in a vision, sure enough, the editors thought that the red ink was appropriate. Because Jesus was speaking to Paul in a *real* vision, right?

Beware the religious bias of translators!

Missing: The Original Gospel Manuscripts

There will always be a dispute about what the gospel authors created—whatever blend of history, folklore, mythology, allegory, and theology it might have been. But New Testament scholars are saddled with another problem as well: *we no longer have what they wrote.* Their original manuscripts did not survive.

So, this is the conundrum. There is no way to know for sure exactly what the original gospel authors wrote. We are at the mercy of much later copies. The copying by hand went on for centuries by scribes who did not have the benefit of eyeglasses or electric lighting. Errors, omissions, and intentional additions were made—by the thousands.

Even if authentic words of Jesus had somehow been preserved in the original gospel manuscripts—against all the odds I've described—the sloppy, haphazard copying process obscures our view. We can't know for sure what the gospel authors wrote. And manuscript detective work has revealed dramatic illustrations of this—two examples:

The first eleven verses of John 8—Jesus defending the woman caught in adultery—which include the words, "Let anyone among you who is without sin be the first to throw a stone at her"[57]—are missing from the oldest manuscripts of John. We have no idea where this story came from. It seems to have been a floater, having ended up as well at the end of Luke 21 in some manuscripts. It's a wonderful story, but we don't know its source. It could very well be a pious invention.

Verses 9-20 of Mark 16 are not in the oldest manuscripts of that gospel, which means they were added later, probably to compensate for the abrupt ending of the gospel at 16:8. And in this fake ending, we find the bizarre promise that baptized Christians will be able to cast out demons, speak in new tongues, pick up snakes, drink poison unharmed, and heal people by touch. It's a relief, I suppose, to know that this is a false attribution to Jesus, but we can still wince. It provides insight into some of the sillier beliefs of the early Jesus sect.

These four obstacles remind us that the "real" Jesus is not within easy reach as has so long been assumed. And they help explain why even the gospel writers could not agree on all the facts about Jesus.

---

[57] John 8:7, NRSV.

12 - Two Versions of Jesus

Here's a two-step challenge that I would expect any follower of Jesus to accept gladly. First, read the gospel of Mark, straight through, without stopping. This will take about as much time as watching a movie. The author of Mark used the word "immediately" 41 times in the gospel. He intended events to unfold in a hurry, so this story of Jesus is best grasped when taken as a whole. Yes, read it in one sitting.

Next, after your immersion in Mark's gospel, have a big glass of wine, then do the same thing with John's gospel. Trust me. You'll need the wine. The fourth gospel will take longer and will be a tougher go. In fact, be prepared for a shock.

When these gospels are read back-to-back, it's not hard to see that their authors had *different concepts of Jesus.* The careful reader cannot help being struck by this. For example, John included lengthy Jesus monologues not found in the other three gospels. (Case in point—see John, chapters 14, 15, and 16.) It's a puzzle: How did Mark—whose gospel was the first to be written, thus supposedly closest to the events described—miss all these words of Jesus? It was common practice in the ancient world for authors to make up speeches for the heroes they wrote about, and it looks like that's what John did for Jesus. But that's not all he made up.

When we compare the first chapters of Mark and John, we could hardly ask for a bigger contrast. If both authors were inspired by God, how did this happen? John was written perhaps forty or fifty years after Mark, which was enough time for theological speculation about Jesus to percolate and escalate.

In Mark, Jesus appears out of nowhere to be baptized by a character patterned after ancient prophets—John the Baptist, who proclaimed "a baptism of repentance for the forgiveness of sins."[58] The author of Mark thought it fitting for Jesus to undergo this ritual—he was human after all. And as Jesus emerged from the water, "…he saw the heavens torn apart and the Spirit descending like a dove on him. And a voice came from heaven, 'You are my beloved Son, with you I am well pleased'."[59] This has been called Adoptionist Theology, referring to the idea that this was the moment Jesus was chosen and then embarked on his career as a peasant preacher, fired with enthusiasm for the imminent kingdom of God.

The author of John's gospel would have none of this. In

---

[58] Mark 1:4, NRSV.
[59] Mark 1:10-11, NRSV.

his first chapter he proclaims that Jesus was present at creation. *Jesus was indeed God's word* through which creation happened:

> In the beginning was the Word, and the Word was with God, and the Word was God. He was in the beginning with God. All things came into being through him, and without him not one thing came into being. (John 1:1-3, NRSV)

Nor would John have anything to do with Jesus being baptized for "forgiveness of sins." John's Jesus never sets foot in the water. Instead, it is John the Baptist who says: "I saw the Spirit descending from heaven like a dove, and it remained on him."[60]

Sometimes we can see Matthew and Luke engaging in their own version of escalating the deity of Jesus. When Matthew absorbed most of Mark and added his "corrections," he positioned Jesus as "Lord at his birth''—as the old hymn puts it—or rather, at his conception by the Holy Spirit. Luke went along with this but expanded the story considerably. He describes pre-birth angel visitations to Mary and her cousin Elizabeth who would give birth to John the Baptist.

The author of John's gospel was sure that Jesus was divine from the beginning of creation and "became flesh"—that was his pronouncement about Jesus appearing on earth. He

---

[60] John 1:32, NRSV.

didn't need a virgin birth to vouchsafe that Jesus' father was God instead of a human. And maybe John's author chose to draw the line here. Virgin births for divine sons were common enough in ancient religions. Borrowing this concept for Jesus may have seemed inappropriate—or simply unnecessary.

Christians over the ages have tended to favor John's gospel because of its dramatically heightened portrait of Jesus. Here he postures as the God of creation, walking among men. But did John get it right, especially when we notice the stark contrast with Mark's gospel? John's escalation, i.e. Jesus=God, should be sufficient warning that his Jesus ***is an invention***. Here was a theologian who was displeased with what Mark, Matthew, and Luke had written. It can be said of all the gospel writers that they wrote theology with little attention to history, but this is especially true of the author of John's gospel.

You may have grown up with John's Jesus firmly in mind—and cherished this version of Jesus in your heart—but I'm challenging you to take a new, honest look at the difference in how Jesus is portrayed in John and the other gospels. The Christian sympathies of scholar Louis A. Ruprecht, Jr. are clear—all the more reason to pay close attention to his analysis of John's escalation of the deity of Jesus. The title of his book should snap anyone to attention: *This Tragic Gospel: How John Corrupted the Heart of Christianity*.

Here's an example of the kind of corruption Ruprecht

writes about. The careful reader of Mark is moved by his description of Jesus' agony in Gethsemane:

> "They went to a place called Gethsemane; and he said to his disciples, 'Sit here while I pray.' He took with him Peter and James and John, and began to be distressed and agitated. And he said to them, 'I am deeply grieved, even to death; remain here, and keep awake.' And going a little farther, he threw himself on the ground and prayed that, if it were possible, the hour might pass from him. He said, 'Abba, Father, for you all things are possible; remove this cup from me; yet, not what I want, but what you want.'" (Mark 14:32-36, NRSV)

But just as John eliminated the baptism of Jesus, he cut the Gethsemane prayer as well, prompting Ruprecht's comment:

> A generation after Mark's remarkable invention of the gospel, John wrote his evangel, as a deliberate attempt to turn Mark's genre upside down and to usurp his place at the center of Christian evangelism. John flatly denied Mark's Gethsemane prayer—or rather, John insisted that Jesus did so—and thus John unwittingly wreaked havoc on Mark's conception of Christian compassion and the 'Christian way.'[61]

---

[61] Louis A. Ruprecht, Jr., *This Tragic Gospel: How John Corrupted*

I have recommended reading Mark and John in one sitting. As you read, here are a few things to be on the lookout for:

- John wanted to heighten awareness of Jesus as a human sacrifice. Mark's Jesus tells his disciples: "For the Son of Man came not to be served but to serve, and to give his life a ransom for many."[62] John is more explicit. He wrote this script for John the Baptist, when he saw Jesus approaching: "Here is the Lamb of God who takes away the sin of the world!"[63] John's gospel was written well after the destruction of the Jerusalem temple by the Romans, which brought a halt to animal sacrifice as a way of pleasing God. Now Jesus alone took on that role. In Mark, Jesus' disciples ask: "Where do you want us to go and make the preparations for you to eat the Passover?"[64] But in John, Jesus dies at the hour the lambs are killed in the Temple, the day before Passover.

- John fails to mention the bread and wine as the body and blood of Jesus in his account of the Last Supper. Instead, Jesus washed the feet of the disciples. The familiar text from Mark,

---

the Heart of Christianity (San Francisco: Jossey-Bass, 2008), pp. 123-124.

[62] Mark 10:45, NRSV.

[63] John 1:29, NRSV.

[64] Mark 14:12, NRSV.

copied by Matthew and Luke, is missing: "While they were eating, he took a loaf of bread, and after blessing it he broke it, gave it to them, and said, 'Take; this is my body. Then he took a cup, and after giving thanks he gave it to them, and all of them drank from it. He said to them, 'This is my blood of the covenant, which is poured out for many.'" (Mark 14:22-24 NRSV) Instead, we find the shocking depiction of the magical properties of eating Jesus' flesh and drinking his blood in John's 6th chapter, following his feeding of the five thousand—as I discussed in chapter 7.

- Just as Mark portrayed a Jesus focused on the message that the Kingdom of God was imminent, with little mention of ethical teaching, so too John's Jesus skipped ethical teaching. He omitted the Sermon on the Mount added by Matthew and modified by Luke. John relentlessly pushes the promise of eternal life and the future day of resurrection—no wonder this gospel became so popular.
- As mentioned earlier, John created scripts for Jesus in the form of long monologues that are missing from the other gospels. Moreover, John had no interest in the popular parables found in the earlier gospels. He simply omitted them.
- While in Mark, Matthew, and Luke, the famous

"cleansing of the Temple" comes at the end of Jesus' ministry, John puts it at the beginning. It has been suggested that Jesus must have done it twice, but why would the earlier authors have failed to mention the first occurrence? This also doesn't work because, in Mark's gospel, Jesus didn't head to Jerusalem until the end of his ministry. But "cleansing the temple" is farfetched anyway. Whoever created this incident in the first place had no grasp of the temple layout: "...the temple grounds were enormous, occupying many acres (the temple as a whole occupied nearly forty acres, and a large portion of that, at least ten acres, was devoted to public space), extensively populated (there would have been *hundreds* of merchants and moneychangers there), and heavily guarded by an armed force deployed to prevent just this kind of thing. They would have killed Jesus on the spot."[65]

- John also portrays *The Jews* as the enemies of Jesus, so much so that his gospel has helped fuel virulent anti-Semitism. Of course, the early Jesus sect was a breakaway Jewish group, which created considerable tension. This commonly happens when religious groups clash. John seemed to have felt a special need to demonize the Jews, for which his gospel

[65] Richard Carrier, *On the Historicity of Jesus*, pp. 431-432.

deserves major demerits. Again, Louis Ruprecht: "One of the many unique qualities of John's evangel is the way he refers to 'Jews' as a people with whom he shares no attachment. Even Jesus seems completely alienated from them. This kind of rhetoric bore a bitter harvest centuries later when Christians came to power and exerted that power against, well, everyone else—but especially against Jews and Greeks."[66] One of John's worst verses is 8:44, in which Jesus addresses the Jews: "You are from your father the devil, and you choose to do your father's desires." (NRSV) Hector Avalos has pointed out that this verse ended up on Nazi road signs.[67] This is reason enough to honestly question John's theology.

- One could go so far as to say that the Jesus of John's gospel is arrogant and egregiously egotistical, another sure sign of deity escalation that should put us on alert. If Jesus actually said, "No one comes to the father but by me," and "The Father and I are one," why on earth would any other gospel writer leave those statements out? The same is true of famous "I Am" sayings—not found in the other gospels—e.g., I am the bread of life, the true

[66] Ruprecht, *This Tragic Gospel*, p. 112.
[67] Hector Avalos' essay, "Atheism Was Not the Cause of the Holocaust," in *The Christian Delusion: Why Faith Fails*, edited by John W. Loftus, p. 378.

> vine, the way, the truth, and the life. Perhaps John's author was thinking of the Ten Commandments in modeling his Jesus, that is, God-the-bully with the opening commandments: ***I am God, don't worship any other gods, don't abuse my name.*** John may also have had in mind Moses' encounter with God at the burning bush in Exodus 3. Moses asked this god what its name was, and was told, "I am who I am." In that era there was a lot of competition in the gods market—well, as there is today—so perhaps the "I Am" sayings were meant to boost Jesus' connection with the God of Moses.

If the story of Jesus is the most important story in human history, and if the message of Jesus is God's once-for-all plan for all of humanity, then why are the different gospel writers so out of sync in their portrayals of Jesus? Why does John, the latest and last of the four gospels, escalate the deity of Jesus and reframe his message? Does all this confusion sound like the best communication the God of the Universe could come up with for the one story, the one overriding truth, that every human should hear, understand, and accept? I don't think so.

Conclusion

Couldn't I just as well have written a book about *Things We're Glad Jesus Taught*? Well, yes, but the feel-good sayings preached from the pulpit—and that end up on greeting cards and stained glass—are well known. Devout folks quite rightly appreciate these, seemingly without even being aware of the negatives about Jesus in full view in the gospels. And there is considerable irony here. One of the best sayings attributed to Jesus has been widely, blatantly ignored by Christians.

> **So when you are offering your gift at the altar, if you remember that your brother has something against you, leave your gift there before the altar and go; first be reconciled to your brother and then come and offer your gift. (Matthew 5:23-24, NRSV)**

In order words, don't even dare to worship God if you're not getting along with someone. I was minister of two parishes, and I soon found out where battle lines were drawn, i.e., the parishioners who can't stand each other. And, of course, there are now more than 30,000 Christian denominations, sects, factions, divisions, and cults. Christians have been fighting each other—even to the point of bloodshed—for centuries. They act like this text from Matthew 5:23-24 should be included in the things they wish Jesus hadn't taught.

Perhaps the Jesus words in Matthew 10:35-36 (NRSV) were more predictive of Christian history:

> **For I have come to set a man against his father, and a daughter against her mother, and a daughter-in-law against her mother-in-law; and one's foes will be members of one's own household.**

And, please, here's additional food for thought. There is so much information about the world and the Cosmos that Jesus could have shared—assuming he was part of God—to improve our knowledge about health and hygiene, among many other things. Once again, we may be told by apologists that Jesus was a man of his times. But surely, if Jesus was "one with God" in any sense, he could have shared insights about how the world really works.

I won't dwell on this, but it ***is*** a problem, given the "trinity" status of Jesus. I suggest readers check out Tim Sledge's insights in chapter three of his book, *Four Disturbing Questions with One Simple Answer*. The chapter is titled "The Germ Warfare Question" and concludes with this:

> "God had been watching silently for thousands of years by the time Jesus came along. It was late in the game, but couldn't the Son of God—the one described as the Great Physician—have made a

> greater contribution to human health than healing a few people while he was on earth? **Why didn't Jesus say anything about germs?**"[68]

But, back to the Jesus teachings that we ***do*** have. Supposedly, the supreme moral test—as suggested by many devout Christians—is **What Would Jesus Do?** From what I've written here, it should be obvious that it's hard to maneuver around all the bad things Jesus taught. Recently evangelical Prophet Jeremiah Johnson faced a backlash of hate from Christians when he admitted he got the word of the Lord wrong when he predicted that Trump would be reelected.[69] Johnson decided to get back to Jesus, so to speak. He announced his intention to focus on "radically obeying Jesus."

Good luck figuring out what that means, but it's such a common sentiment. I recently saw this appeal on a church sign: "Learn to live what Jesus taught." Is that really such a good idea?

I urge Christians to embark on a careful study of the teachings of Jesus in the gospels, but it will take a lot of

---

[68] Tim Sledge, *Four Disturbing Questions with One Simple Answer: Breaking the Spell of Christian Belief*, p. 46.
[69] Hemant Mehta, "Preacher: I Prophesied Trump Would Win Again, But I Must Have Misinterpreted God," *Friendly Atheist* on Patheos.com, January 8, 2021, https://friendlyatheist.patheos.com/2021/01/08/preacher-i-prophesied-trump-would-win-again-but-i-must-have-misinterpreted-god/.

effort and courage. You'll have to move beyond the countless devotional books written by clergy. Instead, explore the works produced by serious scholars, devout and secular alike. So, No, it won't be easy, and if you're a Christian hoping to hold on to the faith, there will be a high quotient of stress.

Will you be able to disprove these observations by three secular scholars?

Dr. Richard Carrier[70] has been blunt in his assessment:

> No, the character of Jesus in the Gospels was *not* the wisest and kindest of beings—he is actually quite loathsome and rarely gives anything but really bad advice.[71]

Dr. Jaco Gericke[72] suggests that the Bible is faith's worst enemy:

> "If you read the scriptures and are not shocked out of all your religious beliefs, you have not

---

[70] See especially, his 600-page book, *On the Historicity of Jesus: Why We Might Have Reason for Doubt.*
[71] Richard Carrier, "What's the Harm? Why Religious Belief Is Always Bad," www.richardcarrier.info, September 10, 2018, https://www.richardcarrier.info/archives/14557.
[72] Richard Carrier, "What's the Harm? Why Religious Belief Is Always Bad," https://www.richardcarrier.info/archives/14557.

> understood them."[73]

Dr. John Beversluis[74] doesn't hesitate to call out the negatives:

> …the synoptic Gospels contain many passages that portray Jesus in a very unfavorable light: behaving with astonishing incivility towards people (including his own mother), exploding with rage, resorting to violence, cursing individuals and sometimes whole villages (and even trees!), threatening people with everlasting torment, instructing his disciples to steal, and destroying a herd of 2,000 pigs.[75]

These statements are so counterintuitive. Why are these scholars so severe? Christians who have been nurtured, since childhood, on an idealized Jesus—learned from pastors and Sunday School teachers—cannot see how these statements could possibly be true. Well, check it out. I encourage all those who wonder "what Jesus would do" to take a close look at the gospels—but an honest look, in

---

[73] *The End of Christianity*, edited by John W. Loftus (Amherst: Prometheus Books, 2011), p. 137.

[74] *Neptune Society of Central California*, "Dr. John Beversluis of Fresno, California, 1934-2021, Obituary," May 22, 2021, https://www.neptunesocietyfresno.com/obituary/dr-john-beversluis.

[75] John Beversluis, Introduction to *The Gospel According to Whom? A Nonbeliever Looks at the New Testament and Its Contemporary Defenders*, Published posthumously on the *Debunking Christianity Blog*, June 29, 2021, https://www.debunking-christianity.com/2021/06/preface-to-gospel-according-to-whom-by.html.

the spirit of rigorous due diligence. Build a list of Jesus sayings that qualify as outrageous, dangerous, or delusional—and another with all the good Jesus sayings you can find. Which list will be longer?

I gave up a long time ago on Jesus as my lord and savior. One major reason for doing so was my growing unease that a loving God would have chosen human sacrifice as a scheme for human salvation. Author Guy Harrison has perhaps expressed it best: "No one seems to know why a god who makes all the rules and answers to no one couldn't just pardon us and skip the barbaric crucifixion event entirely."[76] I was also heavily influenced by my careful reading of the four gospels, as I think I've demonstrated in the first ten chapters of this book. Of course, the gospels are the charter documents of Christianity and fueled its development, but their authors did far more damage to the faith than they ever could have imagined.

---

[76]In his essay, "How to Think Like a Scientist: Why Every Christian Can and Should Embrace Good Thinking," in the John W. Loftus anthology, *Christianity in the Light of Science: Critically Examining the World's Largest Religion*, p. 30 (Amherst, Prometheus Books, 2016).

Dedication

To my kind, generous, outgoing husband of 43 years, David Pandozzi (on the right) who puts up with my scholarly eccentricities: the piles and piles of books, and my disappearance for hours at a time to read and write.

Acknowledgments

One of the hazards of working alone—that's my life as a writer—is that it's hard to perceive that a piece of writing has defects and needs improvement. I thus owe a huge **THANK YOU** to my editor, **Tim Sledge**, who suggested a major refashioning of the original manuscript of this book. Under his patient and persistent guidance, we worked together to put the book into its present shape. Tim saw the book's potential and played an invaluable role in realizing it.

My thanks also to Lois Edwards and Michael Thomas Tower for reading and critiquing the manuscript.

About the Author

David Madison has a Ph.D. in Biblical Studies from Boston University. His strong interest in the Bible began during his teenage years, growing up in rural Indiana in a conservative Methodist home. His parents were not fundamentalists, however, and his mother introduced him to Protestant Biblical scholarship by way of the 12-volume Interpreters Bible.

After graduating from Indiana University, he moved on to graduate school in Boston. But seminary studies, which included theology courses that raised more questions than they answered, had a corrosive effect on his belief in God. This process of faith disintegration continued even as Madison served as pastor of two Methodist parishes in Massachusetts.

He eventually made his escape from the church and pursued a business career. But his fascination with Biblical studies did not diminish, especially since the Bible is a self-incriminating document. He pursued theological reading as well, and after retiring in 2014, focused on writing his first book, *Ten Tough Problems in Christian Thought and Belief: A Minister-Turned-Atheist Shows Why You Should Ditch the Faith*, which was published in 2016. Since that time, he has written a weekly article for the Debunking Christianity website.

https://www.debunking-christianity.com

Madison's concept for this book gelled as he pondered the many negatives about Jesus in full view in the gospels. They're not all that hard to notice, so it's a mystery that devout Christians give Jesus a pass for so many of the bad, mediocre, and even alarming quotes attributed to him in the gospels. These quotes undermine the idealized image of Jesus promoted by the church for centuries.

David Madison may be contacted through his websites.

www.TenToughProblems.com

www.BadThingsJesusTaught.com

www.CureforChristianity.com

You can watch David Madison's video blogs on *You Tube*. Type "David Madison" in the *You Tube* search box to find him.

Bibliography

Avalos, Hector. *The Bad Jesus: The Ethics of New Testament Ethics*. 2015.

Barker, Daniel. *God: The Most Unpleasant Character in All Fiction*. Sterling, 2016.

Carrier, Richard. *On the Historicity of Jesus*. 2014.

Chumney, David. *Jesus Eclipsed*. Createspace Independent Publishing Platform, 2017.

Dennett, Daniel C., and Linda Lascola. *Caught in the Pulpit*. Pitchstone Llc, 2015.

Doherty, Earl. *Jesus*. 2009.

Dykstra, Tom. *Mark, Canonizer of Paul*. 2012.

Ehrman, Bart D. *Jesus*. Oxford University Press, 1999.

Fitzgerald, David. *Jesus*. Createspace Independent Publishing Platform, 2017.

---. *Nailed: Ten Christian Myths That Show Jesus Never*

Existed at All. 2010.

Helms, Randel. *Gospel Fictions*. Prometheus Books, 1988.

Lataster, Raphael. *Jesus Did Not Exist*. Createspace Independent Publishing Platform, 2015.

Lataster, Raphael Christopher. *There Was No Jesus, There Is No God*. CreateSpace, 2013.

Loftus, John W. *Christianity in the Light of Science*. Prometheus Books, 2016.

---. *The Christian Delusion*. Prometheus Books, 2010.

---. *The End of Christianity*. Prometheus Books, 2011.

Louis. *This Tragic Gospel*. John Wiley & Sons, 2008.

Madison, David. *Ten Tough Problems in Christian Thought and Belief*. Tellectual Press, 2016.

Nicholas, Lynn H. *The Rape of Europa*. Vintage, 2009.

Price. *Deciphering the Gospels: Proves Jesus Never Existed*. Lulu Press, Inc, 2018.

Price, Robert M. *The Christ-Myth Theory and Its Problems*. 2011.

Sledge, Tim. *Four Disturbing Questions with One Simple Answer*. Insighting Growth Publications, 2019.

---. *Goodbye Jesus*. Insighting Growth Publications, 2018.

Wells, Steve. *Drunk with Blood.* CreateSpace, 2010.

Witherington, Ben, and Darlene Hyatt. *Paul's Letter to the Romans*. Wm. B. Eerdmans Publishing, 2004.

Made in the USA
Las Vegas, NV
28 August 2021

29089537R00090